DOING
URBAN
RESEARCH

Applied Social Research Methods Series
Volume 33

APPLIED SOCIAL RESEARCH
METHODS SERIES

Series Editors:
Leonard Brickman, Peabody College, Vanderbilt University, Nashville
Debra J. Rog, Vanderbilt University, Washington, DC

DOING URBAN RESEARCH

GREGORY D. ANDRANOVICH
GERRY RIPOSA

Applied Social Research Methods Series
Volume 33

 SAGE Publications
International Educational and Professional Publisher
Newbury Park   London   New Delhi

For information address:

SAGE Publications, Inc.
2455 Teller Road
Newbury Park, California 91320

SAGE Publications Ltd.
6 Bonhill Street
London EC2A 4PU
United Kingdom

SAGE Publications India Pvt. Ltd.
M-32 Market
Greater Kailash I
New Delhi 110 048 India

Printed in the United States of America

Library of Congress Cataloging-in-Publication Data

Andranovich, Gregory D.
    Doing urban research / Gregory D. Andranovich, Gerry Riposa.
        p.   cm.   — (Applied social research methods series ; v. 33)
    Includes bibliographical references and index.
    ISBN 0-8039-3988-4 (cl). —ISBN 0-8039-3989-2 (pb)
    1. Cities and towns—Research. I. Riposa, Gerry. II. Title.
III. Series.
HT110.A56   1993
307.76'072—dc20   93-747

    94   95   96   10   9   8   7   6   5   4   3   2

Sage Production Editor: Tara S. Mead

Contents

Preface

This book was written to provide social scientists, their students, public officials, community leaders, and others interested in understanding our cities with some of the theoretical and practical knowledge needed to conduct research in and about cities. Because we have worked on urban research projects both in the applied and academic fields, we appreciate the need for such a practical guide for those interested in understanding complex urban phenomena and the challenges they represent—for research, for policy making, and for living in cities. With this in mind, we make no pretense about either providing a statistical primer or evaluating the theoretical debates concerning the truth about the urban United States. In the chapters that follow, we suggest general practical guidelines for doing urban research from the types of research resources available to the applied tools needed to conduct your research. Our modest aims are to provide a framework for asking research questions and implementing an applied urban research project—keeping in mind that if the ideas, suggestions, and guides are to be useful, then they must be accessible.

The text takes the reader through the research process, starting with Chapter 1's brief overview of the term *urban* and the field of urban research. Chapter 2 discusses how different levels of analysis can be used in doing applied urban research. Chapter 3 suggests the need for strategic thinking in the applied research process and provides the steps in this process. We believe that thinking about *not only* what you are going to research and how you are going to do it, *but also* how and to whom you will present the research is critical to doing applied urban research. Chapter 4 discusses the issues facing the researcher in designing research projects, including a section on the administrative principles and management techniques that also should be considered elements of applying the design.

In Chapter 5 the focus shifts to data collection, and data sources and research resources are discussed, along with primary and secondary techniques for obtaining data in an urban environment. Chapter 6 discusses the presentation of the research results with communication and use of the research objectives. Finally, Chapter 7 provides a prospectus for urban research, discussing both substantive and methodological issues in the applied research context.

Most chapters are followed by exercises provided to help the reader process and critically assess the information provided in the chapter. We also have offset critical information and provided "how to" examples throughout the text. It is our hope and expectation that this book will help to provide a deeper understanding of how urban research is conducted and the obligations of doing urban research.

ACKNOWLEDGMENTS

This project started in the fall of 1988 after Debra and John's wedding. Special thanks go to Debra Rog (and John Ambrose), Len Bickman, Carol Solomon, C. Deborah Laughton, and Nancy Hale for manuscript and production assistance; Max Neiman, Bryan Jones, and Evans Curry for reading earlier versions of the manuscript; Lou Zweier and the Faculty Computer Lab at California State University, Long Beach (even through the Landers earthquake) for technical assistance and use of the Macs; and Lyndsay McCall of the Faculty Development Lab for Advanced Computing Applications at Washington State University for assistance with the maps.

GREG ANDRANOVICH
GERRY RIPOSA

1

The Nature of Applied Urban Research

WHAT IS "URBAN"?

When thinking about what "urban" means, we are confronted with a number of images, ranging from shining tall buildings, congested expressways, greater opportunities for employment, dilapidated buildings, upscale housing, vacant lots strewn with refuse, community parks, and, most of all, people. Perhaps the images include the stark differences between cultures—African, Asian, Caribbean, European, Hispanic, Middle Eastern—expressing the diversity and cosmopolitan atmosphere of everyday life in big cities. In some cases, the images may be those of opportunity; in others, despair. Historically, our urban images in the United States have tended to oscillate between the positive (cities as innovative, progressive, and modern) and the negative (cities as alienated, pathological, and decadent). Today, popularly depicted urban images include culture, arts and music, recreation and leisure, and the hustle and bustle of commerce as well as violent crime, rampant drug abuse, sharp contrasts between rich and poor, crumbling infrastructure, transportation gridlock, and pollution.

The process of attaching meaning to these images is multifaceted; for our purpose, *urban research* is the systematic examination of the nature of political, social, and economic activities, processes, and outcomes at different spatial levels. The process of urbanization in the United States has resulted in political, social, and economic changes; at the same time, political, social, and economic changes have influenced the process of urbanization. Urbanization is a dynamic process, and its outcomes are seen and felt in different ways within particular cities and across the nation. Consider the recent regional shifts in the U.S. economy, where cities in the so-called sunbelt (South and West) "boomed" and cities in the snowbelt or rustbelt (North and Midwest) languished. In the 1980s, the "Massachusetts Miracle" seemed to buck conventional wisdom, as did the real estate bust in Phoenix, Arizona. But what has accounted for these shifts? What do these broad trends portend? How can the counterexamples be reconciled with the broad trends? (For example, are these cases "blips," that is,

1

anomalies within the trends?) Are these topics even of interest to local, state, or national policy makers? How would the different policy makers define the importance of regional shifts in terms of local political, economic, and social changes? What are the implications of these shifts and changes on particular urban areas? These, along with many other questions, must be addressed by urban researchers.

No precise or commonly used definition of *urban* exists, however (see Box 1.1). Most definitions include an interrelationship between people (demography) and space (political and administrative boundaries, social and cultural arrangements, or economic and technological restructuring). That is, most of the time we think of the metropolis or city or town in conjunction with the term *urban*. The more urban a place, the larger and more diverse its population, their activities, and the spatial area it encompasses. This theme provides us with the broadest focus for urban research: How we learn to cope with the changing interrelationship between people and space can be characterized as *urban capacity*. It seems that a lack of capacity has acted as a catalyst to bring researchers back to study urban settings. In the spring and summer of 1992, violence characterized urban places in the United States and around the world. From Los Angeles to Toronto to Lagos to Meshed, similar patterns of violence erupted. Describing, analyzing, and addressing these problems (and others such as pollution, waste disposal, and homelessness) with a fresh vision is the challenge to urban researchers in the 1990s.

A confluence of political, economic, and social forces has created the current urban crisis of incapacity. The interregional migration of African-Americans and other rural laborers from the South to the North that began in the early 1900s and intensified after World War II changed the social structure of cities and the political demands of city residents (Hawley et al., 1976; Harrington, 1963; Portes & Rumbaut, 1990). Then, federal highway and housing programs accelerated an explosive growth on the city's fringes; this *suburbanization* (the spatial deconcentration of population) resulted in a diminished tax base for cities (Gottdiener, 1986; Lineberry & Sharkansky, 1978). The restructuring of the economy, beginning in the 1970s, which has been characterized by capital flight and low-paying service jobs replacing higher paying manufacturing jobs, brought cities into a period of declining revenues, shrinking economic bases, and a growing unskilled labor pool demanding more social services (Bluestone & Harrison, 1981; Noyelle & Stanback, 1983). Most recently, reduced federal governmental support for our nation's cities in the 1980s has limited political and economic access for many urban residents and has

---

BOX 1.1
The Ambiguous Urban

Trying to define "urban" is not easy. Nevertheless, if we are going to do research in this area, we need some standard definitions to set out our terrain of interest. The definitions below are neither hard and fast nor necessarily the most comprehensive. They are intended to serve as a reference point so that we can communicate more clearly (Herson & Bolland, 1990, pp. 13-14; Baldassare, 1986; Garreau, 1991; Meltzer, 1984).

City: Centers of government and administration, culture, economic enterprise, and social networking often characterized by a dense population (more than 1,000 persons per square mile).

Urban: Spatial land use or organization characterized by dense population, concentrated living space, social networks, and a variety of economic activities and life styles.

Urban Place: A geographic area defined by the Bureau of the Census as having a population of at least 2,500.

Urbanized Area: A geographic area that consists of a central city or two with a population of at least 50,000—plus densely settled adjacent areas.

Metropolitan Statistical Area (MSA): A geographical area that contains one central city or more with populations of 50,000, with surrounding counties that are economically and socially dependent on the central city or cities.

Suburb: Low density, highly populated growth areas on the fringes of the city, characterized by political and economic fragmentation.

Metropolis: The sprawling growth of suburbs has resulted in these multicentered urban areas.

Edge City: Entertainment, shopping, and office areas (multiple-use and mixed-use developments) that have emerged in formerly suburban areas.

Metroplex: Highly urbanized counties, central cities, and contiguous areas that are interconnected economically, politically, or socially.

Exurb: Settlement area beyond the suburbs on the far fringes of an urbanized area (low density, low population).

---

exacerbated tensions (Gottdiener, 1987). The resulting mismatch between problems and resources has led to a crisis—a lack—of urban capacity.

ENTERING THE URBAN JUNGLE

One of the first things discovered through a perusal of the literature covering the urban field is diversity: diversity of topics covered, diversity in the backgrounds of researchers, diversity in methodologies. Oftentimes a single topic is, upon reflection, a matrix of underlying processes and outcomes. Urban economic development, for example, involves examining local political institutions and processes, intergovernmental policies and policy making, regional labor markets and transportation systems, and educational and cultural institutions, among other issues. Each component part, in turn, can provide the theme for different research projects.

The diversity in topics is enhanced by the diversity in disciplinary foci represented by researchers doing urban research. Indeed, the curricula in our colleges and universities include urban courses from a variety of perspectives; anthropology, architecture, economics, geography, history, political science, planning, and sociology departments are well represented, and a variety of interdisciplinary programs also offer urban courses. Each discipline brings its own disciplinary strengths (and weaknesses) to bear on defining the focus of inquiry, be it urban culture, urban form, urban space, urban politics and administration, or urban markets. There has been some convergence regarding the use of theories and methodologies across disciplines in the social sciences, but the sharing of perspectives should not be misconstrued. A number of thorny problems remain within and between different schools of thought regarding basic assumptions, the choice of methods, and the relationship between research and its use (see, for example, Gottdiener & Feagin, 1988; Saunders, 1981; Waste, 1986). The urban field can be characterized as having multiple paradigms: different ways of organizing knowledge and practice in and about urban processes.

Although sharp differences of opinion continue to exist on definition, approach, and emphasis, there has been a basic convergence on the central concerns of urban research. The convergence suggests that urban research should include the characteristics of urban space; the organization of institutions and processes underlying urban political, social, and economic relations; and the linkage of urban centers with one another and with the larger political system, society, and the economy (Sassen, 1991; Smith, 1988). These concerns serve to lend order to the rich diversity of the urban field, while the concept of space serves as the thread that links the above areas of inquiry. Hence the occupancy of space—acquiring and controlling space—provides a means of access to social and economic values (Neiman, 1975; Williams, 1971). Space then takes on a broader social meaning; urban spatial structures and processes are created to control and allocate values (Davis, 1990; Gottdiener, 1985). Questions that begin to draw our attention to the linkage between the use of space and other urban processes are (Lake, 1983, p. xi):

- What is the current spatial form and structure of our urban environment?
- What are the factors and forces that account for the particular structure of urban space, its social and political processes, population distribution, and land use?
- Why and under what conditions do these patterns change?
- What are the consequences and implications for constituent processes?

Our questions, although still necessarily broad at this point, begin to set out a research terrain that focuses the researcher on urban processes without divorcing urban analysis from the characteristics of the broader society. In turn, this allows us to see the interconnectedness of these events and consequences at the local level and link them to transformations in the broader society.

This chapter begins by discussing the concept of *urban*. We then set out the foundations of social science inquiry, focusing on the theoretical issues and their linkage to applied urban research. Urban research without some consideration of theory can lead to identifying only surface events (e.g., homelessness, the recent urban riots) without recognizing the underlying processes that have led to these events. After establishing this basic groundwork, the elements of applied urban research are discussed. As part of this discussion, levels of analysis are introduced as a way of conceptualizing and organizing research strategies. Finally, the chapter concludes with a statement of the goals and organization of the text, as well as a caveat about what the text is not.

URBAN RESEARCH

Urban research is conducted from two general positions. One is academically oriented (basic research) and focuses on theory building. The other is policy-oriented (applied research) and focuses on problem solving. The two positions are not mutually exclusive; the interests of both basic and applied researchers converge in wanting to better understand and improve our quality of life in urban areas. Researchers and research projects can and do easily move from one orientation to the other. There is a benefit to using the methods of basic research in an applied research project and to thinking about the practical implications of conducting basic research. In the subsection that follows, the applied research orientation is more fully elaborated. This is followed by a brief overview of the scientific method, which is the foundation of basic research.

Applied Urban Research

Applied urban research focuses on the processes and outcomes of urban-ization with the goal of acquiring a sharper understanding for policy-making purposes and providing a better quality of life for those of us living in urban centers. Thus applied urban research means the identifica-tion and solution of the problems occurring in urban space. Topics ranging from the support and location of streetlights, parks, and police stations (or substations) to theater, opera, and ethnic festivals are potentially research-able. The researcher must undertake a broader reading of the issue or topic, including not only its theoretical influences but also the experiential influences of the city's inhabitants and policy makers. Linking knowledge to practice enhances the usefulness of research. Doing urban research and doing applied urban research are not separate endeavors; questions raised out of intellectual or pragmatic curiosity and followed by systematic examination are useful for problem solving if the research results can be transferred to policy makers.

Taking this line of reasoning a step further, the process of doing urban research and getting the results of the research used also should not be thought of as separate endeavors. Policy makers, whether in the public, private, or nonprofit sectors, are often interested in the alternate specifi-cation of issues central to their organizational missions, particularly if such specification is provided in an accessible and results-oriented way in a professional language they can understand. Research results become useful when you work collaboratively with the policy maker throughout the project, from designing the methodology to linking the results to policy concerns to resisting the use of jargon. This produces user-friendly applied urban research.

In this light, one primary characteristic of applied urban research is that, in recent times, much of it has taken a policy focus. By *policy focus*, we mean that the research is collaborative, problem-oriented, and conducted to provide potential solutions to geographically bounded urban problems (Lerner & Lasswell, 1951). The components of the policy process are shown in Box 1.2. For our purpose, this draws attention to three important research issues: (a) time and space, (b) comparative studies, and (c) a focus on the relationship between processes and outcomes.

The effects of time and space (or history and place) on urban research cannot be overstated. Because urban areas continue to evolve, what was perceived as a relative nonissue in Seattle or San Diego in 1975 may be of significant interest today (e.g., solid waste disposal). Likewise, for New York City, Cleveland, and other cities, the question of financial solvency,

---

BOX 1.2
The Policy Process

The policy process is the sequence of events that eventually turns public interests into public policy. The stages or sequences of the policy process are provided along with analytical questions pertinent at each stage (for a general discussion of the policy process, see Anderson, 1984; Jones, 1984; for an urban example, see Morgan, 1989, p. 69; Waste, 1989; for doing policy analysis, see Hogwood & Gunn, 1984; Lerner & Lasswell, 1951). Each stage has a "feedback loop" that channels new information back into the policy process, influencing future policy development.

Issue Creation: What gives rise to the issue? How does the issue become defined as a public matter?

Agenda Building: How does the issue reach public decision makers? Who participates in the agenda-building process and how? What keeps problems off the public agenda?

Issue Resolution: How do public officials respond to demands for problem resolution? How is the final policy choice made?

Policy Implementation: Who is involved? How is the policy affected or perhaps changed in this stage of the process?

Policy Impact: What is the result of the policy? Who has benefited? Who has been harmed? How is this assessed?

---

which was of paramount concern in 1975, has taken a backseat to other issues today. Further, the effects of time change not only the relative significance of particular issues, but also our perception of the issues themselves. Homeless people are a concern in every urban center today, but the dimensions of this issue have changed remarkably over the past decade. Homelessness in the past was characterized as an affliction of derelicts, winos, and deinstitutionalized mental patients living on the margins of society. Today homelessness has been redefined to include children, families, and unemployed or underemployed workers who are nevertheless part of mainstream society. This has occurred, in part, because of the shortage of moderate- and low-income housing stock, the result of national housing policy, and the restructuring of global markets (see Hoch & Slayton, 1989). Urban research focusing on homelessness must be cognizant of changes in the population of homeless persons over time in order to address current problems or different dimensions of the problem as well as the forces that have created a new class of homeless persons; after all, the "solutions" for deinstitutionalization or underemployment are different. Planning for services for these homeless people must also consider the deconcentration of the homeless population in urban areas, reflecting the evolving multicentered form of the urban United States.

A second research issue is the need for comparison (Walton & Masotti, 1976). Although there are differences between urban areas in terms of population demographics, political institutions, and economic bases, cities sharing similar characteristics may provide a basis for comparison and generalization. Why are the residents of some neighborhoods or cities more accepting of "LULUs" (that is, locally undesirable land uses, such as halfway houses, fire stations, and prisons) than others? If such a facility is planned, what are its implications? Comparative research helps address these questions. Although it is true, however, that comparative urban research is undertaken more frequently today than 10 years ago, it has not reached a peak yet because of the difficulty in collecting comparable data across different sites. Some of the concerns here are the following: data collection and storage often differs between cities; the reliability of data cannot be easily verified; and the consistency of data across different categories within a single city may be uneven. The costs associated with building comprehensive, cross-city data bases have precluded their widespread development (Clark, 1990). One available and often used alternate source is data provided by the U.S. Bureau of the Census, although these census data also have limitations (discussed further in Chapter 5).

A final research issue is the necessity of specifying process-outcome relationships. One of the more common urban processes is population movement, which occurs at many levels. Within urban areas, people move among neighborhoods and urban centers. Regionally, people have moved from the Northeast and Midwest to the South and West. Although examining population movements to find out where people moved and what the net changes have been is important, the population movement has resulted in various urban outcomes, direct and indirect, foreseen and sometimes unforeseen, that are equally important. For example, urban outcomes associated with population movement include the gentrification of some neighborhoods that displaces lower income residents, increased demands for social expenditures in the central city government, and congested highways. Urban research tends to focus on either category (process or outcome) at the expense of the other with little linkage made between the two. It is our contention that processes and outcomes need to be more closely linked (Riposa & Andranovich, 1988). By linking processes and outcomes, urban research can provide a broader and deeper understanding of issues and their underlying causes, and it also has the potential to suggest different policy choices.

Applied urban research, then, has a collaborative, problem-solving orientation, is conducted in a user-friendly manner, contains findings as well as recommendations on "how to respond," and is often conducted on behalf of an organizational client (government agency, nonprofit foundation, or private corporation) that pays for the research. To accomplish these ends, however, the researcher must include time, comparison, and process-outcome relations in the research strategy.

Scientific Thinking and Method in Applied Research

The challenges urban research holds are many and varied. Armed with some modest tools and an element of creativity, you can be in a position to help explain events that, on the surface, seem impenetrable, thereby enhancing our ability to manage our urban quality of life. Admittedly, this may be a bit dramatic, but the underlying themes still apply: Quality urban research is important and can be challenging, but to produce relevant, pertinent, and timely results, you will need a strategy. And the strategy demands science. Urban research manifests a scientific character when it is valid, compelling, and communicable.

The scientific method provides the process to test theories and hypotheses by applying certain rules to design, data collection, and the analysis of empirical events under strictly delineated conditions. In other words, the scientific method is a mode of inquiry or a way of knowing that has a common language base, resting on the foundations of explicit, systematic, and controlled research (Manheim & Rich, 1986, p. 4). Although different variations of the method exist, the following steps will assist your research (Hoover, 1988; Shively, 1984, p. 1; see also Hedrick, Bickman, & Rog, 1992, in this series).

- Identify the problem and its components
- Develop hypotheses about causal relationships
- Develop variables and measures that fit the hypotheses
- Test the accuracy of the proposed relationship
- Evaluate your hypotheses
- Make suggestions about their significance

We have (re)acquainted you with the tenets of the scientific method to help facilitate the underlying process of doing applied urban research. The formality and the structure of the scientific method should not imply that your research topic cannot be interesting. Following the tenets of the scientific method allows you to: (a) accomplish the goals of your research and (b) contribute to the solution of a problem (applied research) or (c) produce new facts that have a bearing on theory (basic research).

What makes a particular research question interesting is how it relates practice to our knowledge base; thinking theoretically—at a more all-encompassing level—can help develop this linkage. Organizing your research activities (design, data collection, analysis, and reporting) around theoretically informed questions helps clear a path through what otherwise might be a tangled thicket of undifferentiated data. As Shively (1980, p. 3; 1984, p. 2) notes, "defining or sharpening theories gives us a handle on the universe. . . . Reality, unrefined by theory, is too chaotic for us to absorb." Theory helps make sense of the reality of urban processes by providing an opportunity to determine the logical and persistent patterns of regularities in social life (Babbie, 1989, pp. 19-21). Theory helps turn data into useful information.

Suppose you are looking into helping organize volunteers for a social service program in your city after the city council informed city departments to find economical ways of providing services with limited funds. The types of tasks that the volunteers would perform include general office work, computer data entry, bilingual interpretation, library work, and some recreation assistance. The objective is to identify people who will probably stick around as volunteers for a 1-year period. The only data immediately available are files on volunteers to the program for the last 5 years. How will you identify potential candidates? You have just finished reading several research papers on volunteer participation (e.g., Sundeen, 1989) that have shown that higher education levels, marriage, parenthood, contributing money to other causes, and residence in medium-sized cities are positively related to—that is, are good indicators of—long-term volunteer participation. Drawing on this theory, you can now look through the files to see if this profile fits any of your program's past volunteers and then establish a checklist for screening potential candidates for long-term volunteering.

Theory, then, takes a set of events that occur, seeks to find a common pattern among them, provides for generalization concerning relationships, and allows repeated investigation of the same phenomenon. Inherent in the scientific method is the drawing out of relationships between concepts and, more specifically, between variables (a variable has no fixed value; it is an event that varies).

At this point, you are thrust into one of the most important and exciting parts of research: looking for the causal relationships within your study's findings, thus testing theory. Scientific thinking ultimately begins with causal thinking. At the first level of this intellectual enterprise, we can look for co-occurrence or association between our independent and dependent variables; that is, the values of one variable tend to *coincide* with certain values of the other variable (Babbie, 1989). However, causal relationships, while related to association, demonstrate that the values of one variable *produce* the values of the other variable. Theoretical research strives for understanding causal relationships, where theory provides for: (a) an independent variable (one that produces change), (b) a dependent variable (one that is affected by change), and (c) the causal thinking that links the two.

In the above example on volunteering, variables such as level of educational attainment, age, gender, children living at home, income level, home ownership, and city size were important in determining whether a person was likely to volunteer to a public agency. The phenomena that we think will help explain certain behavior (educational attainment and so forth) are called *independent variables.* Conversely, *dependent variables* are hypothesized to be influenced by independent variables. Explaining volunteering (the dependent variable) is not as simple as identifying independent and dependent variables, however. Which variables are important and why still need to be ascertained.

As Shively (1980) notes, a question about whether a relationship exists is objectively testable. However, he warns that causal thinking, although imperative to the research process, is subjective. This caveat suggests that finding a relationship is not the same as establishing cause. With this complexity in mind, we offer two qualifying thoughts: (a) look for the influences that have the greatest effect, and (b) seek to explain the primary causes of that effect at any one time. By using these guidelines to examine the patterns of cause-and-effect relationships, we are able to devise ways of predicting future events, providing a way to influence programs by building this information into their design.

Following through with our example, suppose you interviewed all volunteers for the past 2 years and developed profiles of volunteers based on the independent variables. Suppose 80% of the volunteers who stayed for a 1-year period had at least a college education, were married with children, and contributed money to other causes. Would you then be able to construct a profile for identifying long-term volunteers? What might your checklist look like? Do you think that you could successfully predict whether a particular candidate would make a good long-term volunteer? This type of applied research exercise illustrates the importance of theory and the scientific method for problem solving in the urban setting.

The following questions are suggested as a checklist to assist you in dealing with the complex morass of causality (Meehan, 1988).

- What caused a particular situation to change?
- What was the process of the change?
- What were the outcomes of the change?
- What other variables could have been responsible for the outcomes of the change?

LEVELS OF ANALYSIS

Understanding urban phenomena requires that you make the linkage between activities, events, processes, and their spatial outcomes. For the urban analyst, this means placing the problem and its solution in a spatial (urban) context. For the most part, we tend to examine urban problems within geographic boundaries, be it a neighborhood or "community area," city, special district, labor market, newspaper or television circulation area, sales territory, or even watershed. In each such area, we can develop a list of corresponding problems and potential solutions, but how can we cut through the multiple and overlapping administrative, cultural, and economic boundaries that often exist within a watershed, city, and even neighborhood?

The concept of levels of analysis provides one method of linking solutions both to and across spatial hierarchies (see King, 1990; Smith & Feagin, 1987). As we move along the hierarchy of the spatial scale from neighborhood to the world urban system, the relationship between contextual forces and the city changes. Levels of analysis, therefore, provide "markers" that help focus and sharpen the research design, data collection, and data analysis. Selecting from among the different levels of analysis, while acknowledging the interrelationship between the levels, permits the researcher to examine urban phenomena in ways that illuminate the details of a particular problem or issue within the context from which the problem emerged.

We discuss levels of analysis more fully in Chapter 2; at this point we would like to offer five levels of analysis useful in doing applied urban research: neighborhood, city, region, national system of cities, and world system of cities. Of course, the topic of your applied research, the specific questions, and the needs of your client will determine at which level(s) you conduct your research project.

The task of this monograph is to assist the researcher in the applied urban research enterprise. We neither discuss the merits of various theoretical frameworks in uncovering the "truth" about the urban United States nor explain the application of specific statistical techniques discussed more thoroughly elsewhere (e.g., Babbie, 1989; Welch & Comer, 1988). Our aims are more modest and limited to providing a framework for asking research questions and implementing an applied urban research project. In the following chapters we suggest guidelines for doing urban research. Chapter 2 continues the discussion of how different levels of analysis can provide useful markers in doing applied urban research. Chapter 3 suggests the necessity of strategic thinking in the applied research process. Chapter 4 discusses the issues surrounding the design of research projects and includes a section on the administrative principles and management techniques that can be derived from the design.

In Chapter 5 the focus shifts to data collection, and data sources and research resources are discussed, along with primary and secondary techniques for obtaining data in an urban environment. Chapter 6 discusses the presentation of the research results focusing on communication and use. Finally, Chapter 7 provides a prospectus for urban research, discussing both substantive and methodological issues in the applied research context.

Most chapters are followed by exercises provided to help the reader critically assess the information provided in the chapter and to practice some of the strategies and techniques discussed in the chapter. We have also offset critical information and provided some "how to" examples throughout the text. Like the other volumes in this series, this monograph is aimed at first-time researchers (undergraduate and graduate students), "old timers" entering a new arena, local public officials who are interested in finding out more about how research is conducted, and nonprofit institutions whose members are involved in urban affairs. It is our hope and expectation that the following chapters will help in providing a deeper understanding of how urban research is conducted, and the obligations of doing urban research.

EXERCISE

Note: The exercises throughout this text are designed to promote discussion and presentation. Our premise is that applied urban research, as a human enterprise, demands reference work but also benefits from informed discussion. Thus the exercises have an implicit format: read, look-up, discuss in small groups, present (either verbally or in written form), and debrief. A useful debriefing process is "journaling": writing down your personal assessment of what took place. For example, what did you see? What was your initial reaction? After thinking about it, what have you concluded? Did you learn any lessons—substantive and methodological—that might be used in the next exercise? We encourage you to think about the exercises in two ways, substantively about your topic and about the process of working in teams. Because so much of life involves teamwork and the topic is so neglected, the exercises have a process goal: learning how to "team."

Divide your class or seminar into teams and assign both of the following exercises.

1. Members of the team will go to the library and draw on scholarly, applied, and popular sources to develop a conceptual map of the local "urban." Bring these findings to the next meeting and discuss them with your team, at which time you will attempt to settle on one definition and present your perspective to the class.

2. Review the last week or so in your city's newspaper or a major metropolitan newspaper. What are the major urban issues facing the city or metro area you have selected? Take one of these issues and identify its primary research question. In your team, work this question through the scientific method: (a) What are the independent and dependent variables? (b) How do they vary? (c) How do the variables relate to the facts in the story? (d) What causal thinking is evident in the story? Present your assessment to the class for critique.

2

The Urban Setting: Levels of Analysis

In the last decade urban research has taken a global turn. The importance of linkages between cities and their environment has been recognized as critical to the understanding of urban phenomena at the end of the 20th century (Henderson & Castells, 1987; King, 1990; Smith & Feagin, 1987). From neighborhood to region to world system, urban processes affect the form of urban space and how we see and think about urban phenomena. Researchers have started to explore new process-outcome linkages such as the reliance and implications of using technology and security systems in urban areas, the loosening of spatial ties, and the influences of postmodernism that have resulted in a consumption-oriented urban development, particularly in industrialized nations (Harvey, 1989; Sorkin, 1992). These new linkages have called for the development of different substantive questions that describe the evolving patterns of urbanization, the relationship between urban areas and the global economy, and the changing relationship between people and urbanization. At the same time, urban researchers are applying different research methods to address these linkages, often relying on multiple methods (such as secondary data analysis, surveys, and ethnographies) to bring out the details of urban phenomena (e.g., Gottdiener & Pickvance, 1991). Because of the importance of this contextual orientation within the urban field, we have focused this chapter on levels of analysis. Our purpose is to affirm the importance of this new contextual orientation and to encourage urban researchers to think about how seemingly specific urban issues are derived from and also contribute to larger global changes.

Levels of analysis focus and sharpen the research design, data collection, and data analysis. Again, note that selecting from among the different levels of analysis permits us to examine urban phenomena in ways that focus on the details of a particular problem or issue within the context from which that issue emerged. This is an important tool because urban phenomena are products of specific courses of action or inaction undertaken by various actors (e.g., individuals, governmental institutions, and private interests large and small) at the local, regional, national, and even global levels.

In the next section, we define the concept of levels of analysis. In subsequent sections, we first identify the characteristics of the different levels of analysis and then provide examples of research questions and variables from the vantage points of the different levels. Integrated throughout the chapter are heuristic examples of urban research done at these different levels.

WHAT DOES "LEVELS OF URBAN ANALYSIS" MEAN?

Ordinarily, when people think of *urban*, the city comes to mind. When thinking about urban phenomena and the multifaceted dimensions and questions that ensue, can we realistically consider urban to be the exclusive domain of the city? Certainly, cities do make up a large share of the emphasis in the term; cities historically have been the focal points that bind urban space. However, focusing exclusively on cities in urban analysis would unnecessarily exclude important aspects of a fuller, richer conceptualization. Thus we suggest that the urban analyst think of the urban area as a mosaic of neighborhood, city, region, national system of cities, and world system of cities.

Levels of analysis refers to the spatial interlinking of urban places. The urban system is characterized by political, social, and economic processes occurring at the local, regional, national, and global levels. In applied urban research we can therefore think of levels of analysis as providing a hierarchy of problem-solution frameworks mediated by governmental or nongovernmental institutions.

Each of these levels represents an opportunity to assess problems and problem-solving properties at different levels of the spatial (urban) hierarchy. We will deal at length with each level individually later. Still, consider how each level contributes to the understanding of urban phenomena and how the levels of analysis help us to understand how urban phenomena are interlinked. Research design, data collection, and data analysis are derived from how a particular research project is conceptualized within the context of levels of analysis.

The examination of proposed development in San Diego—a new airport, for example—could proceed along several lines, depending upon which level, or levels, of analysis are most important to the client (see Figure 2.1). How does proposed development affect *cities* in the south county? How will the fast growing north county *region* be affected by longer commute times for air travel? How does San Diego's *twin city* of

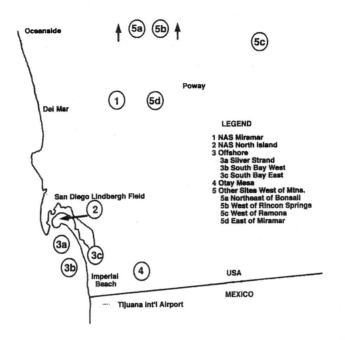

Figure 2.1. Potential Airport Sites

Tijuana, Mexico, fit into the equation? How will this affect the flow of commercial investment capital coming into *Southern California* from Asia? The relationship between the levels of the spatial hierarchy—the south county, all of San Diego County, San Diego, and Tijuana, or Southern California's (from Los Angeles to the Mexican border and beyond) position in the Pacific Rim—suggest a hierarchy of problem-solution frameworks that might be used to address the implications of developing a new airport.

The research design (your applied urban research strategy) for each of the above questions would change depending on the specific question asked. The research design must account for different variables, causative agents, data availability, and the purpose of the research. A north county business association might be interested in how the added commute time would affect small businesses, while a south county business association might be more interested in how increased congestion would affect commercial traffic crossing the international border. A research project sponsored by a regional business association might look at both questions; in each instance, the research design would be affected.

Data collection and data analysis would be similarly affected by the level of analysis used. Transportation data collected at the city level of analysis can help define changes in commute times that affect small business travel that occurs during off-peak hours. If you were collecting transportation data at the regional level of analysis, however, you would need to note small business and commercial flows as well as the environmental impact of these flows. Data collection would include indicators of regional and crossborder traffic and measures of environmental (air basin) effects. The scope of data collection and analysis would be different at the city and regional levels of analysis.

Two points should begin to materialize from this overview: (a) An urban issue can occur at various spatial levels, and (b) different spatial levels offer different opportunities to understand related but different dimensions of a particular urban issue. Two caveats must be addressed briefly at this point. Applied urban research often is grounded in placeness (e.g., the city) and is addressed in *spatial* and *temporal* terms. At the root, however, are several analytical concerns that must be addressed. Because much applied urban research is problem oriented, care must be taken to maintain empirical validity when moving between levels or when examining one variable at several different levels. As we move along the hierarchy of the spatial scale from neighborhood to the world system of cities, the nature of contextual forces changes in terms of their intensity, complexity, and diversity requiring the exercise of great care on our part to ensure that our conceptualization of forces (e.g., actors, processes, environments) influencing spatial arrangements is consistent with the scale used.

In temporal terms, urban phenomena at various levels of analysis may not seem to change much at the time of a particular research project, masking the continuous flux and longer term change that is more easily measured over time. Most urban databases rely on cross-sectional rather than longitudinal data, which can create a problem. When we conduct longitudinal analyses but use data bases that were collected at a single point in time, we must realize that we have substituted a series of snapshots of urban events or activities because we do not have a video record of those events or activities. This technique is often used, however, given the absence of longitudinal data and the difficulty of (re)creating these data.

CONCEPTUAL TOOLS FOR URBAN ANALYSIS

Because of the difficulty in understanding inherently complex urban questions, we will add two more tools to help you identify, order, and clarify the activities occurring at different levels of analysis: the concepts of *provision* and *production*. These two concepts can help the applied urban researcher link spatially differentiated processes to outcomes, helping frame and reframe seemingly disparate complex phenomena.

Provision suggests Lasswell's (1938) "manifold of events" in which a political process influences the organization and decision-making process of government or society that results in an allocation of scarce public values. Provision not only implies government action, but also, and just as important, highlights issues such as channels of access (formal and informal), the structure of competition and collaboration, and the organization and communication of interests. This lens allows the researcher to examine neighborhood coalitions, city government, special districts, and even street gangs and to delve into the ties that bind and affect the neighborhood, city, or region.

Production refers to the private sector's organization and the means and methods by which it conducts its business affairs. Production points to more than manufacturing and services; today it refers to the development of highly specialized services (e.g., financial services, legal services, real estate and architectural services, and advertising and insurance) and top-level management needs (e.g., communication and control). Sassen (1991, pp. 325-326) notes that production is an important focus for urban research partly because it highlights the *site* of production, effectively linking cities to the urban hierarchy. Through this lens, we are able to investigate the points and arrangements of production and consumption, their influences, and biases as they are played out in the urban hierarchy. Now let us see how these concepts work at different levels of analysis.

Neighborhood Level

At one end of the spatial hierarchy is the neighborhood. In the broadest terms, a neighborhood is a cluster of residences right around one's own home (Herson & Bolland, 1990, p. 158). Usually, neighborhoods have some dimension of homogeneity based on ethnicity, housing type, market values, or social and cultural values. As these dimensions (or variables) change, we note a distinction between different neighborhood communities (Zehner & Chapin, 1974). We are alerted to the existence of important quality-of-life processes that affect provision at the neighborhood level.

Neighborhoods are responsible for much of the pressure at city hall (Yates, 1980, p. 178). Neighborhoods are the locations for struggles over economic development (Kantor & David, 1988, p. 244), points of tenant organizing and neighborhood leagues (Lawson, 1986), and "flashpoints" or scenes of urban riots. More broadly, neighborhoods are the placehold-ers of community values that influence local governance over the myriad urban policies implemented in or affecting a city. Each perspective sug-gests that the neighborhood can be a useful level of analysis for applied urban research focusing on the underlying urban social or political pro-cesses (Blakely, 1979; Green, 1985).

Downs (1981) underscores the rich vein of research awaiting the urban analyst interested in neighborhoods and implicitly underlines the value of *provision* as an analytical concept at this level of analysis. According to Downs, the neighborhood manifests three traits: (a) Its common space is a focal point for interpersonal interaction; (b) it binds common relation-ships with some nearby institution, such as the church; and (c) it has the characteristics of common membership or common identity. These traits contribute to building a foundation of interests that can become an impor-tant part of local decision making. The ebb and flow of these interests, within and among neighborhoods, affects the cohesion of neighborhoods and ultimately their political and sociocultural efficacy both within the neighborhood and beyond (at the city level, for example).

Many neighborhoods have experienced traumatic changes in the past decade. In some cases, only poor people now live in a neighborhood; or, conversely, speculators and developers have gentrified blighted areas, displacing the previous residents (Barry & Derevlany, 1987; Smith, 1979). In both cases, the character of the neighborhood changes socially, eco-nomically, and politically. Neighborhood residents feel themselves under siege from crime, a rising cost of living, and a seemingly unresponsive local government. These factors have combined to reduce social interac-tion as the basis for neighborhood life (Herson & Bolland, 1990, p. 159). In response, neighborhoods have become locations for political organiz-ing (Henig, 1982; Hiss, 1990; Williams, 1971).

Another response that falls within the provision process is neighbor-hood-level mechanisms for promoting security, access, and exclusion. Examples range from gated communities to main street associations, neighborhood associations, and street gangs (Herson & Bolland, 1990; Williams, 1971). Each mechanism, although seemingly different from the others, is a way of organizing and securing its members' cohesion and efficacy. Ultimately, these associations politicize the struggle to control the development of urban space.

For example, the Neighborhood Open Space Coalition, made up of 125 neighborhood organizations, succeeded in working together to create a 40-mile bike and pedestrian path from the Atlantic Ocean to Long Island, New York, called the Brooklyn-Queens Greenway (Hiss, 1990). This policy response, although needed in one of the most congested urban regions in the United States, came about only after a long struggle with city officials and developers who had other land uses in mind.

Neighborhoods are the site of diversity within a city. Different neighborhoods represent different parts of the larger urban mosaic, reflecting the variety of issues and concerns that are important to different groups who live in the neighborhoods. Still, you can identify some of the most salient issues to neighborhoods. Among these are crime and drugs, the quality of public education, opportunities for youth, police-community relations, the investment in locally owned businesses, coping with neighborhood transition (either gentrification or residential succession and the quality and affordability of neighborhood housing stock), availability of and access to health care, revisions in traffic circulation patterns, and homelessness.

The following indicators are just a few examples of how these issues might be addressed quantitatively:

- Demographic indicators
- Household incomes and property values
- Housing stock (number of owner-occupied units, rental units, and abandoned units)
- High school graduation rates
- Crime statistics
- Number and type of citizen contacts
- Statements at city council meetings

Data sources other than population data from the federal government might include:

- City council meeting minutes
- Records in the city clerk's office
- Annual reports from neighborhood-based associations
- Memoranda from the office of the city's ombudsman
- News media (contrast larger newspapers with locally owned and operated newspapers or with the city's *Reader*)
- Zoning maps from the city's planning department
- Investment records for neighborhoods targeted for reinvestment
- Precinct voting data

The City

Cities are the urban places that have captured the most pronounced attention in urban analysis, in part because they are the centers of government and administration. Critical areas for investigation are health care, education, police and fire services, housing, crime, drug abuse, employment, and tax base issues. The question now becomes how to analyze urban processes and outcomes at the level of the city; the city has become so commonplace in our lives that often its complexity is obscured by its familiarity. Contributing to this is the evolution of multicentered urban places in which "the city" becomes several spatially distinct urban centers (e.g., Knox, 1991).

Using the city as the level of analysis first requires defining it and then applying conceptual tools that delineate its dimensions, functions, and its role within the urban spatial hierarchy. From this the researcher is able to reduce the city's complex social organization into more manageable parts to grasp what this level of analysis can provide.

One difficulty in defining the city is that it resists any one exclusive classification; rather, it suggests an interconnected web of social, political, and economic attributes (Herson & Bolland, 1990). Thus cities are centers of cultural activities, economic enterprises, and social networks. This leads to the city's most important attribute, one that differentiates the city from other urban places: Cities are points of government and administration.

Cities are also important points of economic production and consumption within society's economic fabric (Tabb & Sawers, 1984). Even with the much discussed capital flight to the suburbs, exurbs, and beyond, cities continue to be the location of choice for advanced-producer service centers (e.g., financial and legal services), heavy and light manufacturing enterprises, and warehousing and distribution hubs. This relationship between our cities and the nation's mode of production is hardly new or earth-shaking; cities have been central to U.S. economic development since the colonial period (Benjamin, 1984), and the meteoric development of the world capitalist economy has generated the growth of the modern metropolis (Gordon, 1984). Still, the connection between the changing spatial patterns and relations and the transitions in the capitalist economy make production an integral vantage point at this level of analysis (for richer discussions of this transition, see Gordon, 1984; Riposa & Dersch, 1992; Smith & Feagin, 1987; Tabb & Sawers, 1984).

Understanding these transitions within the economy and their attendant consequences for cities, you can investigate the spatial patterns in the division of labor. Cities can be categorized for the purpose of comparison (Riposa & Andranovich, 1988), and conclusions concerning how cities contribute to neighborhood, national, and international economic conditions can be drawn. Conceptual questions along the production dimension at the city level of analysis include the following:

- What role does a particular city play in economic processes (production and consumption)?
- How is the city's spatial form conditioned by its role in the economy (e.g., finance center, service center, manufacturing center, and administrative center)?
- What are the economic linkages between cities?
- What are the effects on households (jobs, housing, and income) and the community (schools and other services)?

Nevertheless, overemphasizing the concept of production can lead the researcher to technological determinism or economic determinism, with urban changes explained solely in technological or economic terms. A more comprehensive analysis demands the inclusion of other elements, such as politics and culture, thereby allowing the researcher to analyze urban change as the product of a social struggle, not an outcome of "nature" (Gottdiener, 1986; Tabb & Sawers, 1984). Failure to employ an integrated approach to the analysis of the city might lead us to find that politics does not matter in city policy making, a much-debated conclusion in Peterson's analysis of urban economic development policy (Peterson, 1981; Stone & Sanders, 1987).

To analyze the provision dimension and its relationship to production, the operation of economic interests or groups in the city must be examined. This includes not only the formal interest groups that vie for influence or which are excluded, but also the administrative agencies that formulate and implement local policy.

One extremely useful way of examining the city as a center of government and administration is through the *regime* paradigm (Stone, 1989). Regimes include the nomenclature, behavior, and biases of formal organizations, as well as "the informal arrangements by which public bodies and private interests function together to be able to make and carry out governing decisions" (Stone, 1989, p. 6). Browning, Marshall, and Tabb's (1984) study of political incorporation underscores the relationship between formal institutions and informal coalitions in influencing government responsiveness. To use the regime approach to analyze the city, the following questions are suggested to guide your design, data collection, and analysis:

- How are interests organized by the political process?
- Who participates in the governing coalition?
- Who directs the governing coalition?
- How is the governing coalition held together?
- What difference does the coalition make in urban policy decisions?
- Whose interests are ultimately served?

A second approach in operationalizing the concept of provision is *urban managerialism* (Block, 1980; Pahl, 1975; Saunders, 1981). Urban managers are those persons who hold positions of authority within public organizations and play an important gatekeeping role in the process of provision. Through discretionary authority, urban managers regulate access to scarce resources and control the distribution of public services. The following questions are example probes that are relevant to the examination of provision at the city-level of analysis:

- Who are the important urban managers in your study?
- Are they elected or appointed?
- What are their attitudes toward your urban policy question?
- What drives their power? What is the extent of their power?
- What values guide local administration?
- What managerial role does the dominant urban manager manifest in executive leadership?
- Who makes up the dominant coalition or regime?
- What is its relationship to the city's public bureaucracy?
- How do the spatial conditions of the city constrain urban managers?
- How do the primary urban managers mediate the contradictory pressures of economic development and social services?

Service Delivery

Service delivery ties urban managers to questions concerning government responsibilities. This area of inquiry is useful for understanding policy outcomes that generate political conflict at the city level of analysis. Thus the urban researcher conducting applied analysis often analyzes some aspect of service delivery. Examining service delivery requires that we link government services with performance and access indicators of efficiency or effectiveness. You can use the following variables to examine distribution and access (see Lineberry, 1984; Mendenso, 1986):

Cost of service—expenditure per service rendered;
Location of service facilities—proximity to client population;
Frequency of service—number of services per week;
Condition and quality of facilities—attractiveness or physical condition;
Quality of service personnel—background, demeanor, and client satisfaction;
Service provider to client ratio—proportion of service providers per 1,000 population in city; and
Consumption of services—number of services used.

Assessing the quality of services has proven to be a difficult task, however. Unlike the private sector (where profit maximization is the well-known bottom line), performance in the public sector is difficult to measure. A variety of indicators have been used to get at the issue of service quality, ranging from *input* indicators (i.e., the level of resources committed to a particular program), *workload* indicators (i.e., the "body counts"—numbers of, tons of, gallons of), *efficiency* indicators (e.g., output per some standardized measure such as per capita or per hour), and *effectiveness* indicators (e.g., how well a particular service program has met its goals or objectives).

These variables will help you draw conclusions about efficiency and effectiveness and, to some degree, equity. Levy, Meltsner, and Wildavsky (1974, pp. 16-17) suggest that equity is an important consideration in service delivery questions, one that demands an approach sensitive to the local political and cultural climate. Before assessing equity, the researcher must ascertain how the city has defined this concept. Three types of equity are:

> *Equal opportunity*—all residents receive the same service;
> *Market equity*—residents receive services roughly proportional services to their tax liability; and
> *Equal results*—allocations based on residents being in equal conditions after the money is spent and the programs implemented (sometimes characterized as "leveling").

Once the equity principle has been ascertained, you are then in a position to evaluate whether the city is living up to its own principle and whether this principle actually equates to some sense of fairness.

Mladenka (1989) provides a useful example of one way to assess the distribution of service delivery. Using longitudinal analysis (data gathered at different points in time) and multiple indicators (multiple independent variables), Mladenka measured the distribution of parks and recreation services in Chicago. He employed indicators such as the percentage of population under age 18 and median family income for indicators of need, and used percentage of home ownership as an indicator of service demand. Finally, he used percentage of African-American population as an indicator of racial composition. Mladenka's use of these indicators to assess the equity of service distribution provides a good example of utilizing applied research to examine a "squishy" concept (equity) at the city level of analysis.

The Region

To this point, we have looked at the two more common levels of urban analysis: the neighborhood and the city. Over the past 20 years, however, with the growth of urban places, *metropolis* and *region* are terms that are more frequently encountered and are sometimes used interchangeably (Dickinson, 1964; Shanahan, 1991). Regional processes are often associated with metropolitan areas, where an interdependence of economic ties, social and cultural networks, or political and administrative agreements provide the glue to bind the geographic region (Markusen, 1987). Often this results in a hierarchy of regions that follows the hierarchy of cities (Beauregard, 1989a). In part, this stems from the myriad effects of the spatial growth of cities. The history of the urban United States for the past several decades has been geographic enlargement; larger political and administrative boundaries, more extensive social concerns, and more far-reaching economic ties are characteristic of the urban United States at the end of the 20th century.

The regional level of analysis includes more than a city (either central city or city-suburb or multicentered metropolitan area). *Region* is a spatial term that indicates a broader space for analysis; regions can be as small as a county (the San Diego region) or as large as several states (the Southwest region of California, Arizona, New Mexico, and Nevada). But for most analyses, selecting the region will be determined by your research needs. Production and provision still can provide a useful conceptual framework for examining urban dynamics and actors at this level of analysis; the calculus between these functions has not changed based on this level of analysis.

At the regional level, we become concerned with which urban services lend themselves more to economies of scale than to diseconomies of scale. This has been a critical question in regional policy studies since the late 1950s (Bollens & Schmandt, 1975). By their scope and scale, some services are more amenable to regional solutions than city-by-city solutions, as illustrated in Table 2.1.

More commonly referred to as *transboundary concerns* (which describes a situation of spillover effects or externalities whose effects are felt outside the immediate transactional arena), regional analyses in today's NIMBY (Not in My Back Yard) climate may encompass a state or contiguous states. Regional "solutions" have come to dominate the debates on many of our more pressing social issues. Whether the issues are homelessness; drug violence; crime; the quality of drinking water; the provision of health care services; or the protection of shorelines, wetlands,

Table 2.1
Regional Versus City Concerns

Regional Concerns	City Concerns
Growth management	Health
Airports, highways, transit	Hospitals
Sewerage	Education
Water supply	Fire and police
Sanitation	Housing and urban renewal
Public utilities	Parks and playgrounds

or environmentally sensitive areas, regional approaches are looked at from the perspective of the provision of services to the organization of solutions (Shanahan, 1991).

The production focus at the regional level offers the researcher the lens to view transitions in economic development, such as agglomeration and decentralization and their outcomes, and the consequences of the emergence of a service-dominated economy. Focusing on production at the regional level of analysis can include the examination of manufacturing; retail and sales; natural resources; resort and retirement facilities; and universities, knowledge, and information centers.

The significance of this type of urban analysis lies in the nature of the questions that may be framed concerning the changing (i.e., multicentered) spatial form of urban areas. As the above discussion has illustrated, there is a need to include the larger processes of socioeconomic development in applied urban research. For example, in California, Oregon, and, more recently, Washington, coping with the effects of growth (i.e., growth management) has become more of a regional than a city exercise. Inherent in growth is the rise of some areas and the decline of others; coping with these different aspects of growth requires assessing uneven regional growth (e.g., economic, demographic, and natural resource use), and urban policy responses must account for these differences (see Carney, Hudson, & Lewis, 1980; Perry, 1987).

To accomplish these ends, the critical variables that need to be included in a region-level analysis are the labor force; investment trends; demographic trends; education levels; and several economic characteristics, such as types of businesses and industries in the region, business start-ups, and capital availability and flight. Quality-of-life indicators such as the availability and accessibility of cultural and recreational amenities, the housing stock, airports and transportation, and the existence of negative externalities (pollution, crime, and blight) should also be included. In terms of policy responses, there are a range of possibilities reflecting more or less formal organizational and resource-sharing relationships. Some of the more formal arrangements are interlocal agreements and contracts; less formal contacts include councils of government and ad hoc task forces.

In the future, research at this level will intensify as the regional experience of coping with the growing scope of problems facing cities becomes elevated to the regional level. The lack of regional databases, especially databases that have complete and comparable regional data, is a concern for conducting regional-level analysis (Pivo & Rose, 1991; see Balachandran, 1980).

National System of Cities

At the national level, cities are affected by national goals established for purposes beyond specific urban concerns. As an example, Presidents Ronald Reagan and George Bush followed a "national urban policy" that was driven by a concern for the development of the national economy and wherein cities received less direct aid and were encouraged to become more competitive to attract investment (this trend was sometimes derided as "fend for yourself federalism"). But general policy guidelines, including incentives and constraints adopted during policy formulation and adoption at the national level of government, do have effects on cities and urban policy making (Markusen, 1987). At this level of analysis, the elements of provision and production play a fairly equivalent role, alerting us to the reciprocity existing between politics and economics at the national level. In general, there are three approaches to understanding national influences on urban policies: (a) following the money trail, (b) focusing on federal issues and priorities, and (c) assessing the underlying values and interests of federal decisions.

To ascertain the general direction of urban policy from the national perspective, it is best to rely on the secondary analysis of government documents such as the president's national urban policy report and other Department of Housing and Urban Development (HUD) documents. Among these HUD documents are its annual report, the *Consolidated Annual Report to Congress on Community Development Programs*, the *Bibliography Series*, and the *Survey on Housing, Prices, and Mortgages*.

More specifically, following the money trail leads to a focus on the national urban policy priorities and can be determined from those programs funded by federal grants-in-aid. There are several types of grants (from narrowly defined categorical grants to more discretionary block grants), and their mix is important at the local level. The dilemma posed by these grants is that they are often accompanied by mandates that describe how the funds will be used; such provisions may skew local policy agendas and reflect the interests of national constituencies rather than local interests (Neiman & Lovell, 1981, 1982). This is one of the primary dilemmas that can be addressed at the national level of analysis in applied urban research.

One approach for examining the impact of federalism on urban policy as suggested by Peterson, Rabe, and Wong (1986) follows a public choice framework. Particular locales value some programs more than their costs, and thus they select various grants over others. To protect their economic positions in today's competitive urban arena, cities often are forced to give extra priority to grants that subsidize development of policies. Thus Peterson et al. (1986) suggest that the way to understand federalism and urban politics is to delineate between developmental policy (policies to improve the community's economic position) and redistributive policy (policies that benefit those in need). To use this analytic approach, the researcher must examine the city's policy agenda and link the uses of intergovernmental revenues to local concerns.

A second way of assessing the national system of cities is the issue-oriented approach. Consider the linkages between urban policy and national economic policy, as evidenced by the late Republican regime. From a national standpoint, urban policy is a small part of our overall economic policy. Although there has been a debate over whether the United States has or needs an industrial policy, there was targeted investment in high technology industries via defense policy. This underscores the often overlooked role of the Department of Defense in the spatial development of the United States (Kirby, 1992). Research has shown that targeted investment has had very real spatial effects on patterns of urbanization, particularly in the post-World War II era (Beauregard, 1989b). By focusing on those sectors of the economy that the U.S. government chose to support—in this case, the high technology sectors supported by defense funds—you can assess city-suburban development and uneven development across cities and within regions; like the federal grants-in-aid system, issues of importance to the national economy act to skew local urban policy agendas.

Perhaps a more comprehensive approach that allows us to draw upon the provision conceptualization is the *benefits coalition*, an approach that focuses on the values and interests underlying either the issue-based approach or the money trail. Anton (1989, p. 32) defines the benefits coalition as any group or association of individuals who mobilize, support, and implement government benefits programs. Federal policy, according to this author, is the patterned interaction of any benefits coalition. Analyzing this interaction identifies the bridge that links local urban issues and is concerned with federal policy. Further, it underscores the collective decision process through coalition building at the local level, an essential element of the provision function. Consequently, if the researcher chooses this approach, federalism becomes a system of interest group competition and a system of distribution. To operationalize Anton's approach, the following process is suggested. First, identify and define the benefits associated with the program. Second, identify the distribution pattern associated with the benefits. Third, identify the source of the benefits (such as the enabling legislation and implementing regulations). Finally, identify other groups who may be competing for the benefits. These four components help identify the stakes in specific urban policies, their underlying interests, and how local governments solicit and obtain resources to implement local urban policy agendas.

World System of Cities

Cities exist within a system of nation-states and the global economy and are influenced by economic growth and development, as well as political and cultural movements. The concept of a world system of cities is of relatively recent origin and has grown out of several distinct research traditions (Chase-Dunn, 1985; Hall, 1984; King, 1990). As a result, the core of the concept of world cities remains loosely defined. The importance of this concept for applied urban research, however, lies in the growing interdependence of nations and cities. World cities hold a distinct place in a nation's system of cities as a result of their role and functions in the global economy.

Put simply, a world city can be identified by its political power and economic trade with a concentrated population density; a world city also may be a political capital and center for international corporate headquarters. There is a hierarchy of world cities based on their comparative advantage within the world system of cities. Operationally, this is manifested in the international division of labor. As the international economy has grown more differentiated and sophisticated, world cities have become more reticulate in their roles and functions, engulfing greater numbers of cities in their spheres of influence, regardless of size. There is no single prototype of today's world city, but a profile of characteristics ought to be useful in distinguishing their position within the international system. Some of the characteristics of the roles and functions of world cities as administrative and control centers are the existence of advanced producer services such as education, research, and development; strategic planning and facilities management; banking and insurance; accounting, legal services, and advertising; and real estate (King, 1990; Sassen, 1991).

Because of the importance of world cities to the international economy, these cities have been characterized as international centers containing head offices, branch offices, and regional headquarters such as New York, Paris, and Zurich. At the next tier of the hierarchy are the zonal centers that serve as links in the international financial system and which are dedicated to geographical zones on a lesser than global scale, such as Los Angeles and Hong Kong. At the third tier are the regional centers that are home to corporate headquarters and play a more important role in traditional economic sectors (such as manufacturing) than the advanced service sector; cities in this tier include Chicago and San Francisco (see Hall, 1984; King, 1990; Timberlake, 1985).

Some of the variables associated with world cities studies are regional unevenness, importance of interstate systems, cultural differences, division of labor in the world economy, peripheralization of particular economic sectors (e.g., textiles), reorganization of the service sector (high- and low-paying jobs), key developmental issues creating tensions between developed and developing nations such as immigration policies and population shifts, and the subsequent social costs that tend to exceed a city's capacity to pay (Sassen, 1991; Timberlake, 1985). These variables highlight the production focus at the level of world system of cities.

Although this level of analysis may not be of general utility in many applied urban analyses, there are specific cases in which some of these variables may play an important role in policy formulation. Understanding the role and impact of the global division of labor and international investment patterns provides an important context for recognizing the linkages and relationships of interdependence in the global economy. One such example of this interdependent relationship is found in transboundary manufacturing in the San Diego-Tijuana metroplex, in which policy makers must contend with rapid growth, an influx of unskilled labor, and illegal border crossings—in San Diego and Tijuana—and the costs of coping with the social consequences (Andranovich, 1991; Herzog, 1986). Drawing upon a world cities perspective, the applied urban researcher has the opportunity to reframe many of the urban questions that ordinarily are defined within the context of city or regional jurisdictional or administrative boundaries. Recognizing the interdependence of cities fosters a concomitant understanding of the processes underlying urban interdependence, thereby encouraging a more holistic view thus soliciting a wider range of policy alternatives.

SUMMARY

Levels of analysis provide a useful way of framing or reframing your applied urban research questions. This chapter has examined how different levels of analysis provide different avenues of understanding urban phenomena rather than providing an excursion into the well-rehearsed field of statistical techniques. We provided a conceptual framework distinguishing between production and provision functions occurring at five levels of analysis. We understand that these levels of analysis are not mutually exclusive; given the interrelatedness of urban space and its role in national and international economies, this is unavoidable. Nevertheless, we have demonstrated that different levels of analysis can provide different types of information to the urban researcher. One ought not see these levels as providing disparate pictures but rather as presenting a holistic portrait that often is viewed from different angles and through different lenses.

EXERCISE

In this chapter, we focused on using levels of analysis as an applied urban research tool. If you are in a classroom setting, the whole class can do a "futuring" or environmental scanning exercise (see Morgan, 1986) that focuses on issues that are in your city's future. After the class generates its list of issues through brainstorming (either individually or in small groups), these issues can be clustered into similar categories based on level of analysis. Each group could then:

1. identify the applied research questions for a single cluster;
2. identify stakeholders and their levels of influence in problem solving;
3. identify the level at which the cluster's "opportunity" or "problem" could be resolved (and why it should be);
4. consider the linkages between the different levels of spatial hierarchy in your city and their effect on solving urban problems; which issues seem more likely to be resolved and why?

3

Preparing for Applied Urban Research

This chapter provides an overview of the urban research enterprise. Urban research often requires bringing different disciplinary perspectives, methods, or modes of exposition to shed light on urban phenomena. Our goal is to link applied urban research to the research process. For many first-time researchers, making this linkage can be a daunting prospect, but it becomes much easier and less difficult the more practice one gets. One of the factors underlying this fear is that urban research is multiparadigmatic—that is, there are several different frameworks that can be used to help understand how and why urban processes unfold and to identify and explain their outcomes.

The topics covered in this chapter help bring a strategic, applied approach to the research process. We use the term *strategic* because it suggests such questions as "What is the purpose of the research?" and "How can it be best accomplished?" If these two preliminary questions are not examined systematically and with great care, your research project can quickly turn into a research bog. Other strategic concerns include how ethical issues affect the research process (such as what the researcher owes the client or those involved as research subjects) and what can be done to ensure that the research results will be used. These concerns provide the researcher with an opportunity to gain an overview of the context of the research before actually initiating the project.

In the first section below, we present the big picture and address strategic questions that serve as a guide for substantive, methodological, and even personal choices. Next we discuss certain obligations of the researcher that also should be part of the initial strategy: sponsorship and control, the accuracy and confidentiality of data sources, and the disclosure of methods. The final section of the chapter deals with enhancing the potential of applying research findings.

THINKING BACKWARD

It is helpful to consider what the final results of the research might show, which analytical frameworks may be employed, and how both your research needs and the needs of the client or sponsor might be met. Making certain choices rather than others about research framework, data collection tools or analytical techniques, or the presentation of the results does affect the future conduct of the research, so it is important to consider all of these components together before launching your research project. Addressing these issues in a systematic manner before starting out is what we mean by thinking strategically about applied urban research; this is also a good way of taking an inventory of the knowledge and skills you have going in and what you will need to do on a particular urban research project.

One way of thinking strategically is to think of the completed research product and then picture all of the steps necessary to achieve its completion (that is, think backward). This should not be strictly a mental exercise; writing down the steps you envision gives you not only the advantage of total recall but also a starting point for incorporating many of the administrative details of research. Therefore, one way to think backward would entail making a list starting from the bottom of a page and working toward the top (starting at the top of the page is okay!). Such an exercise should include several different types of information, such as:

- Defining the scope of the research
- Identifying variables
- Considering different levels of analysis and causal relations among variables
- Identifying potential sources of data
- Estimating data collection needs
- Taking an inventory of the resources needed to proceed
- Considering the ideal (most rigorous) research design
- Identifying potential findings
- Targeting your audience and determining how you will present your findings

At this stage you are brainstorming the ideal way to do the research (see Box 3.1). Constraints of existing data sources, time, or money imposed by any particular data collection or analytical strategy should be delayed for later consideration.

To assist you in thinking backward, consider the following guideposts:

1. Make a quick determination of what you know about the issue. Can you pull out the issue's central ideas or themes? If you have received a request for proposals (RFP), can you identify an area of need and then focus on how to research it? If you are on the other side of the table (looking for research on a particular urban issue), can you define your

BOX 3.1
Thinking Backward About an Applied
Urban Research Project

The city manager has just called and asked you to conduct a study about the extent of and constraints on economic and political incorporation of minorities—African-Americans, Latinos, and Southeast Asians—in the city. To get started on the project you retreat to your office or favorite spot for rumination and begin thinking backward. You can start at the bottom of the page; for clarity, we began at the top.

1. *The presentation of the final report* (which will detail the extent, including the driving and constraining agents, of minority incorporation). Specifically, the report will provide the city manager and later the city council with ethnic group comparisons on a series of variables that suggest economic and political incorporation: population, income levels, poverty rates, home ownership, unemployment rates, job occupations, business ownership, bankruptcies, voter registration and turnout, minority campaigns for public office, minority office holders, and level of neighborhood organizations. The report must be accessible to the layperson because it will be presented at a public city council meeting and then released to the media.

2. *Writing the report.* I will write the first draft and then circulate a copy of the drafts to several colleagues and the city manager for comments. Enough lead time will be allowed to include any last-minute data or corrections. Tables, figures, and graphs will be needed to clarify the findings; the information services department will provide the graphics.

3. *Analyzing the secondary and primary data.* The secondary data will include academic and government reports for context and baseline data (e.g., income, employment, and voting registration). Primary data will consist of field interviews with minority leaders and activists of the minority community, street-level bureaucrats, and locally elected officials. Descriptive summary statistics will be used to analyze the secondary data. Primary data will be assessed for insider viewpoints and perspectives concerning economic and political incorporation in the city.

4. *Conducting field interviews with local officials and community activists and leaders.* Interviews will be conducted individually, face-to-face, and will emphasize the character of economic and political incorporation in the city. Interview times and locations will be prearranged and interpreters will be contacted as necessary.

5. *Pretest of the field interview protocol is conducted with one city council member, one community leader, and one street-level bureaucrat.* The pretest determines if the open-ended questions can draw out the needed information from the respondents. Continued scheduling of field appointments.

(Continued)

BOX 3.1
Continued

6. *Identify the sample frame for the interviews.* Target local officials that have decision-making influence in the incorporation area. Compile a list of community leaders from the newspapers, references from other community leaders and local officials, and names appearing in the city council's meeting minutes. Construct the questionnaire in consultation with peers and a university professor that studies incorporation at the urban level.

7. *Collection of secondary data from local agencies, university, and nonprofit organizations.* Some leads on collecting these data are as follows. Voting data can be obtained at the city clerk's office; business data can be obtained at the community development office and the chamber of commerce; block census data can be obtained at the city's information service department and the local university in the computer center; and background literature on each ethnic group can be obtained at the local university library. Start the interview-scheduling process.

8. *Identify secondary data sources and locations.* Talk with the client for leads.

9. *Choose the design strategy for your research project.* Identify possible variables (population, income levels, poverty rates, home ownership, unemployment rates, job occupations, business ownership, bankruptcies, voter registration and turnout, minority campaigns for public office, minority office holders, and level of neighborhood organizations). Compare data collection techniques given the type of project, the goals of the research, and its time frame and resources.

10. *Literature review.* Review academic material at the local library. Call the department of sociology or political science for the name of a professor who researches this area to give you a few leads. Review will provide identification of research completed on the topic and suggest approaches.

11. *Decision about staffing, time, and cost.* "Ballpark" it: Make general estimates of time and cost to help you decide whether to follow a full-blown design or opt for a quick and dirty approach.

12. *Call from the city manager soliciting your assistance to research economic and political incorporation in the city.* Your first question to the city manager is "When do you need this by?"

needs clearly and in simple terms so that a variety of alternatives can be generated to address these needs?

Once the central points have been identified, consider the nature of the following questions. What is already known? What has already been done? Who are the best contacts for further information? If you have the time, a quick literature review and telephone calls to persons knowledgeable about the issue might be warranted. If not, at least make a list of some key words and the names of potential contacts. The question of information availability and accessibility is critical to thinking strategically about research. These steps help develop your understanding of the topic itself.

2. *Identify how you might approach the topic.* Is there time and are there resources to conduct a full-blown research project or is a "quick and dirty" approach suitable? This affects the methodology employed as well as the generalizability of your results. If you can conduct a full-blown research project, the choices available are limited only by your imagination and resources. If you have pressing time constraints or are working under severe resource limitations, an alternative might be needed. Often the "quick and dirty" approach is dismissed as practiced solely by flimflam artists. In fact, time is often a most pressing constraint, and missing a deadline means that all of your work will have been for nothing. Using a "quick and dirty" approach should not necessarily suggest shoddy work. Remember that doing applied urban research is different from conducting academically oriented research (i.e., developing and testing hypotheses and building basic knowledge). Besides having a deadline, utility of results is a goal of the research. Given the vast amount of data already available on most issues in most urban areas, shortcuts should be part of the strategic thinking process. Patton and Sawicki (1986) lay out an extensive path for beginning urban policy analysts to follow based on the premise that good work can be done expeditiously. Moreover, good research lies less in the length of time to completion than in how you do it, given resource availability and the constraints under which you are operating.

3. *Identify outcomes.* Applied urban research needs to be action-oriented. This means not only looking at process but also linking process to outcomes. This linkage allows you to build action-oriented responses into your problem-solving research. Three questions can help you identify some of the most important outcomes in your strategic thinking process: (a) Who benefits? (b) Who is harmed? and (c) What needs to be done to achieve the outcomes? Reviewing these questions will provide an idea of the scope and scale of a particular applied urban research project.

4. *Personal needs.* Lastly, you should consider what you will gain from becoming involved in a particular research enterprise. Interest in the topic and the development of your conceptual and technical skills should play some part in your decision to undertake or participate in a research project; your interest also should help to determine your role in the project. If your interest in a particular research issue is high, then you are more likely to

be motivated to pursue this topic. This seems obvious, but if you are interested in policies to mitigate the effects of violent urban youth gangs in public schools, then doing urban research on shelter alternatives for the homeless might not be appropriate. Doing research is also a personal activity based on your own interests, knowledge, skills, and professional needs. There are no hard and fast decision rules to help sort such choices. We offer two suggestions, though: First, if you do not know anything about the topic or the method to be used, do not get involved in a key position; second, if you are finding it more and more difficult to keep track of your home, office, or car keys, you may want to ask yourself whether you are overextended.

Levels of Analysis

A strategic overview of the research enterprise requires thinking about which level(s) of analysis to employ as well as the implications of such choices on data collection and analysis. As the next chapter points out, there is a linkage between design and levels of analysis. The question of focus (on the neighborhood level, the city level, or the regional level) has serious implications for research design. Alternatively, are you interested in events within a single city, in several cities, or between cities? These questions can only be answered in the context of specific research questions.

For example, there has been a longstanding concern with illegal border crossings along the U.S.-Mexican border (see Figure 3.1). But what is the best way to research this urban issue? In San Diego, California, this issue erupted in a series of events in 1989-1990, including a "Light Up the Border" campaign (citizens protesting border violence after dark showed up to shine lights on well-known illegal crossing areas), a task force of the San Diego regional council of governments (SANDAG) examining the nature of transborder issues in the greater San Diego metropolitan area, a major effort by CalTrans (the state highway department) to increase motorists' awareness that people were crossing freeways and running the risk of being fatally stricken, and in national news coverage of American youths playing "war games" along the border at night and harassing Mexican nationals. In this complex case, several different levels of analysis might be utilized to provide several different perspectives on the nature of the border-crossing issue. It is extremely important to be clear about the particular context within which the issue is examined because each level requires a slightly different research focus. A regional focus may look broadly at the border from the Pacific Ocean to Otay Mesa, from the

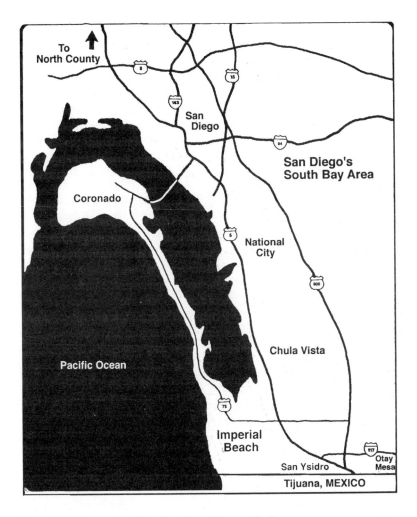

Figure 3.1. International Border, United States-Mexico

Mexican border to San Diego's north county, examining a host of issues and outcomes such as jobs and social service provision, while a city focus would take a narrower look at more localized effects such as policing, streetlighting, and nightly helicopter monitoring.

The selection of the level of analysis represents a strategic decision that may govern all aspects of the research enterprise. Each level of analysis represents different choices for identifying and selecting variables and establishing causal relations among variables, as well as having implications for data sources, data collection and analysis, and the generalizability of results. How would you conduct an applied research study to address the issue of illegal border crossings if CalTrans or SANDAG provided you with funding for a 1-month study? How about a 6-month study? What if the City of Imperial Beach asked for research on illegal crossing along the beach for the next city council meeting in 2 weeks?

Thinking About Design

The key to strategic thinking at this stage of the research process is to help think through choices that would get as much descriptive or explanatory power out of the research design as possible without losing contact with reality. All designs make certain assumptions with which the researcher must then live; these can take the form of yielding to certain value positions, holding certain events constant, or simplifying some conditions. For example, value assumptions can lead the researcher to assume that experts ought to play a greater role in decision making or that public participation has a positive affect on urban policy outcomes. By conceptualizing certain events as constant or unchanging, the researcher might assume that only certain conditions or types of behavior produce certain outcomes. Finally, the researcher might simplify conditions to isolate the independent or primary causative agent, assuming, for instance, that the very existence of a community health clinic improves community health.

Think of the role of assumptions in a different way. Suppose you are studying the factors underlying violent urban street gangs in your city. If you start with the assumption that gang behavior is deviant behavior, then you would develop a research design that focuses on the psychology of the individual. However, if you take a different tack and assume that gang behavior is driven by culture conflict, then your research design necessarily would focus on groups and how the lack of social mobility and social discrimination affects their behavior. Thinking backward allows the researcher to identify the role that assumptions play in shaping the research design.

It is safe to say that there are no simple cookbook approaches to applied urban research, and the testing of theory and reality can occur in a variety of different ways. But, as you might suspect, the selection of different approaches must not be made willynilly. There should be compelling theoretical and methodological reasons for bringing different approaches to bear on a particular issue, and the use of multiple methods in applied urban research is quite common (for a general treatment, see Mark &

Shotland, 1987; Yin, 1989; for a neighborhood-level treatment, see Mayer, 1984, Appendix B).

By bringing different approaches to bear, however, you run the risk of obscuring the results of the research and the utility of your work. The principles of Occam's razor—simplicity, predictability, and importance— should help guide strategic thinking. Simplicity is related to comprehension: If you cannot explain to your client what you want to do, then your research may not be appreciated (and probably not used). Predictability is a linkage concern: Your design must relate theory with observation through time. There are many different ways of doing this, depending on the context of the research question and time and resource availability. Importance is related to the usefulness of your applied research: Does your design provide information relevant to the needs of your client? Is it action-oriented, providing your client with potential response strategies?

Summary

Adopting a strategic approach—thinking backward—to applied urban research gives you several important and useful research tools. First, strategic thinking provides a systematic approach to assessing research opportunities. This thinking process will help you:

- Identify the client's critical research questions
- Assess the advantages and disadvantages of different approaches
- Inventory existing or known data sources
- Identify linkages to outcomes
- Link theory to observation

Second, the strategic thinking process is a form of creative, collaborative problem solving that is closely tied to the context of specific urban issues and forces a consideration of critical and relevant questions. Third, strategic thinking is a way of prioritizing needs, generating alternatives, and selecting the alternative that can address the client's needs in the best way possible.

OBLIGATIONS OF THE RESEARCHER

Using a strategic approach in urban research, as with the research enterprise in general, compels the researcher to conduct the study in an ethical fashion. There are a variety of resources available to help you address ethical concerns (for a richer discussion, see Kimmel, 1988; Sieber, 1992; both are in this series). The critical responsibilities required for the conduct of research are dealing with informants, misrepresenting or extrapolating beyond the data, and presenting the methodology. Much more difficult is the issue of recognizing your personal biases and how they might affect the conduct of your research.

The issue of how to deal with informants is central to applied research. Whether you are conducting fieldwork or a survey, you are involving people. The treatment of human subjects is governed by strict guidelines if you receive funding from a public-sector agency and should be explicitly addressed in all urban research projects. How the researcher represents the study to informants or respondents is an important component of the management of the project, particularly if several researchers and data collectors are involved. To ensure the integrity of your research, it is important that the process be as open as practicable.

Confidentiality is another strategic concern. Confidentiality or the protection of informants or respondents is vital to the conduct of frank interviews and honest responses. From a strategic standpoint, it may be helpful to think of sample designs that help to maintain confidentiality (see Henry, 1990; Marin & Marin, 1991; both are in this series), such as relying on more than one informant or respondent for critical information.

From a strategic perspective, it is also necessary to consider how to present your research so that it can be used by the client. This step also allows the research to be evaluated and replicated. All aspects of the design (sampling procedures, data collection procedures and protocols, and the rationale underlying these) should be included in your thinking about presentation. A critical component of this is the full disclosure of the methodology.

One common problem faced by decision makers is how to interpret and use information in decision making (Weiss & Bucuvalas, 1980). As researchers, we tend not to think of the constraints under which decision makers operate. While we worry about the generalizability of our findings given the methods used, decision makers are more interested in the findings and suggestions for response strategies. Therefore, plan to present your methods with a consideration for your reader's needs. Do not fall into the academic habit of using *statisticsh* (relying on jargon and in-house understandings of complex formulas): Your research report may be ignored or relegated to a position of importance on the window sill under a plant.

Misrepresenting and extrapolating beyond your methodology and your data are two cardinal sins. You are obligated to analyze and discuss your findings within the limits of your method and the boundaries of your data.

For example, if you are using descriptive statistics (frequencies, cross-tabulations), then you are using techniques that do not permit you to predict. The use of large data sets, such as census data, and multiple indicators raises the risk of mistaken reporting. Nonetheless, the responsibility falls on you to present your method correctly and your analysis accurately.

A more difficult concern is philosophical: You need to consider the consequences of your research, because, as a researcher, you have little control over how your research will be used. A well-known example of this is the development of atomic weapons in the 1940s. After the bombs were used as police instruments, the scientific community was divided over the use of this research. A more local example can be found in the area of criminal justice policy. Research has shown that saturation policing can contribute to the reduction of violent street crime and drug trafficking in high crime neighborhoods. To obtain these outcomes, cities have adopted this policy but have interpreted the concept and research findings in different ways, leading to different applications. For some cities, this policy means an increased police presence in the community; for others, it has served as a rationale for aggressive behavior toward neighborhood residents (see Davis, 1990; Riposa & Dersch, 1992). The lesson for applied urban research is to consider whether your personal interests and values can be reconciled with the prospective project *before* you get involved.

ENHANCING THE USE OF THE RESEARCH

Utilization is the goal of most applied urban research. As such, utilization should be of primary concern to the researcher. The topic of utilization has spawned its own field of research and its own journal (*Knowledge*), which has contributed to a better understanding of what it takes to get research used in the decision-making process (see Ball & Anderson, 1977; Weiss & Bucuvalas, 1980; Yin & Andranovich, 1987).

Because this is the topic of Chapter 6, here we will only briefly build on the opening point made by Majchrzak (1984) in her discussion of communicating policy research to policy makers: that communication is a two-way process requiring the researcher to keep decision makers apprised of the constraints and realities of the research process as well as informed about how information may be useful at future times. Communication is an important part of doing valid applied urban research. At the same time, the decision maker should let the researcher know the constraints and realities of his or her world, as well as how anticipated changes might affect the research. The importance of this point goes beyond having two-way interaction; it suggests that researchers and informed decision makers (or clients) must rely on each other and work together.

The informed client will want to be involved in every aspect of the research process. You will be provided with a certain amount of focus in terms of understanding your objectives, approach and method, and reporting strategies. You should address all of the client's concerns, both procedural and substantive, to get your research used; after all, you must be responsive to the client's needs. Some clients may want to review all data collection instruments or protocols. Even if the client does not, you should insist. In addition, as Palumbo (1987, p. 20) points out, many programs have political goals as well as substantive goals. Applied urban research requires sensitivity to these nonresearch goals; all of this must be explicitly incorporated into your strategic calculus.

Finally, it is critical to present your research in a timely manner; timely not only to meet externally imposed deadlines, but also to provide clients with fast, quality information (Weiss & Bucuvalas, 1980). Full-blown research designs may have to yield to more adaptive ("quick and dirty") approaches. Again, the purpose, approach, method, and reporting strategies must address the client's needs. One way to ensure utilization is through client commitment to the research, and working together is the cement for building commitment. Carol Weiss (1984) suggests making utilization a focus of your research (see Patton, 1986).

SUMMARY

The central theme of this chapter concerned strategic thinking as the essential underpinning for applied research. Often omitted or ignored, this process calls attention to the scope, design, and administration of the project. For example, thinking backward—a method of bringing strategic thinking to your research project—allows you to penetrate the surface of your project, delve into its nuances, and help construct a more rigorous research design. Using this process holds the promise of reducing the costs of doing applied urban research. In short, strategic thinking provides an early reality check.

EXERCISE

Select an urban issue in which you have an interest, have discussed in the previous exercise, or have considered for a term project or paper. Examples are eliminating drugs and weapons in local schools, building more affordable housing in the city and reversing capital flight from the core city, and increasing minority participation in local elections and decision making. Break into small groups and practice the strategic overview process by doing strategic thinking. At the end of the exercise, write down your observations of the group process: What worked? What did not work? Why? This process can be done in two steps. First, spend 5 minutes working individually on thinking backward. Then spend about 20 minutes working together as a group. Next, pull your strategy together for presentation to the class.

To get started, consider how you are going to research this topic of interest by thinking backward, elaborating as much as possible along the way during this preliminary stage of the research process. Push your discussion on the potential research process to its limits; remember, you can act on every question or aspect you think of now. Later, you will have to simply double back or exercise damage control. Include in your strategic thinking process which level of analysis will be selected and why. Will your research project require any special obligations on your part? If so, what are they and how will you deal with them? Now synthesize the points and justifications from the discussion for presentation to the class and submission to the instructor.

4

Research Design

Broadly speaking, a research design is the strategy that guides the process of collecting, analyzing, and interpreting data (Manheim & Rich, 1986, p. 88). It notes the target population, process-outcome relationships, and levels of analysis you want to study, and it organizes the research process into a format that allows systematic observation and timely reporting. Design follows function: Your goals and research purposes will dictate different design strategies. As was discussed in the previous chapter, strategic thinking is a valuable method for the early clarification of the research goals and purposes that are integral to any design strategy. At a general level, given the action orientation of applied urban research, different research designs provide direction in choosing from among alternative techniques for data collection and analysis. As you read this chapter, however, keep in mind that there is no one "right" research design.

BUILDING BLOCKS FOR THE RESEARCH DESIGN

From the exercise of developing a strategic overview of the research project, we know that the research design will be based on developing research questions. The first step in research design is asking general information questions. The following is a checklist of general information questions (Putt & Springer, 1989, p. 81):

- How much information is known about the issue (who, what, when, how, why)?
- What type of problem is the research expected to address?
- What do the stakeholders (e.g., client, decision maker, target population) wish to do with the information?
- What is the importance of the issue in relation to other issues?

Once you have ascertained these basic information needs, you should then move on to more substantive questions and to the development of your analytical framework. Suppose, however, that you are still unsure about the specific substantive questions upon which to focus. Developing an analytical framework is futile without an idea of what these questions might be. If this is the case, a quick reminder of what applied urban research is about can help: Urban analysis as an applied activity (collaborative, problem-oriented, alternative-generating) seeks to help policy decision making improve our quality of life. Remember that applied urban research focuses on the political, economic, and social conditions that influence decisions concerning the match between scarce resources and competing and escalating demands. Therefore, focus on these conditions to derive your substantive questions.

An analytical framework is the approach that is taken to examine your research problem. It is important in the research design process because at this point you specify the target population for research, identify variables and measures, determine levels of analysis and the causal relations among variables, and develop possible designs to operationalize your research question. In developing this framework, you are encouraged to use your right brain (logic and deduction) as well as your left brain (imagination and speculation). The following tools are helpful in the development of your analytical framework (Meehan, 1988, p. 54).

Concept—a notion or idea used to organize our perception;

Proposition—statements that relate two or more concepts to one another;

Variable—something that takes on different values and allows different levels of measurement;

Conceptual framework—a set of concepts or variables that experience has shown to be required for dealing with certain kinds of events and activities;

Hypothesis—statement that predicts a relationship between an independent variable and a dependent variable;

Unit of analysis—objects being studied, such as individuals, cities, or governments;

Operationalization—deciding how to measure your variables for analysis, including whether you are looking for association or causes;

Generalization—inference, or whether your findings can be replicated under similar conditions (applied urban research, however, can be idiosyncratic, focusing on problem solving in specific localities); and

Theory—a set of propositions that suggests why events occur and provides reasons for the causal linkages among your variables.

These tools are derived from scientific thinking and represent the ideal analytical framework. Hypothesis testing and generalization may not be relevant in a particular applied research project, where the results of an investigation are focused on resolving specific problems rather than accounting for categories of events. The latter is the task of basic research.

HOW TO CHOOSE YOUR RESEARCH DESIGN

You should base your choice of design on the function or purpose of your research. Research designs are not mirror images of one another. Each has its own strengths and limitations (see Cook & Campbell, 1979). To select the appropriate research design you must first ascertain: (a) your time, staffing, and funding needs; (b) information availability and accessibility; and, most important, (c) the purpose for your study. We cannot underscore enough the importance of ascertaining these needs—particularly purpose—before the selection of your research design. Generally speaking, applied urban research is undertaken for one of three purposes: exploration, description, or explanation.

Exploratory Research

Suppose you are asked to examine and analyze the prevalence of violent urban street gangs in transition neighborhoods or the role of neighborhood healers in community health service delivery. In the first case, the phenomenon is fairly recent; in the second, although the phenomenon is old, it has rarely been examined. Both examples capture the essence of exploratory urban research. Your purpose is to develop more information about the nature of the issue (Putt & Springer, 1989, p. 87).

Your task, then, will be to define the scope of the phenomenon. Because you do not have exact knowledge, you are interested in casting the research net broadly, emphasizing breadth to identify the basic dimensions and characteristics of the phenomenon. This may later lead to either a descriptive or explanatory research project. For now the goal is to gain more familiarity with the phenomenon so that you can formulate more precise research questions about the processes and outcomes that are potentially associated with it.

A large measure of exploratory research demands creativity. The lion's share of this process will be tailored toward talking with others who have experienced the phenomenon in question. To assist you in doing exploratory research, consider the following approach:

- Review available studies and records
- Brainstorm with colleagues
- Brainstorm with people in the field who have experience
- Conduct a series of selected interviews with the research subjects

This process enables you to fill in the context in which the phenomenon is occurring—and to do it quickly. More important, it directs you to discussing the phenomenon with informed sources through brainstorming or interviews.

Descriptive Research

Descriptive research plays an integral role in applied urban research. It takes a clear step beyond exploratory research in that it provides a more clarified, context-oriented perspective of the research terrain (Manheim & Rich, 1986, p. 69). Now the objective is to focus our understanding. The objective will be to derive empirical data on the characteristics of particular urban conditions, such as neighborhood responses to NIMBY facilities, service coordination versus service integration, or developing public-private partnerships for economic development.

For example, suppose you are examining the relationship between drug abuse and youth in your city. This explosive issue has been on the urban agenda for the better part of two decades and has been the subject of numerous basic and applied urban studies. In spite of this previous work, your task is to develop a more precise understanding of this condition as it exists in your locale today (e.g., neighborhood, school district, city). You could begin by collecting data on the number of (a) youth arrests for drugs; (b) students reporting drug use in high school; (c) students attending drug counseling in high schools; (d) school expulsion rates for drug abuse; (e) telephone calls to drug crisis intervention centers; (f) youth in treatment programs; and (g) the perspectives of drug counselors. The purpose of descriptive research is clarification; in the example provided, the purpose is to clarify the context of drug abuse by youth in a specific urban locale.

Two criteria are necessary to increase accuracy and precision in descriptive research. First, the research design must include accurate measures of the concepts and variables; second, the design must include a method for selecting reliable and unbiased data. Thus descriptive research requires creativity in selecting your indicators and measures. You can create a useful portrait of the research subject using baseline data and multiple indicators of the phenomenon, as illustrated above. Previous studies can provide excellent clues in terms of how to begin, potential measurement problems, and knowledge gaps resulting from particular approaches. By using well-known and generally accepted indicators, the validity of your description is enhanced.

Statistical analysis may be possible in this type of research. For example, using summary statistics (e.g., measures of central tendency, frequency distributions, scatterplots) is an excellent way to portray the characteristics of the phenomenon under examination. However, this still leaves you short of being able to venture any solid theories about what might have caused the phenomenon. To reach that point, you must first understand the frequency of the problem or phenomenon and what other factors might be associated with it. Then you will be ready to build toward explanatory research.

Explanatory Research

Explanatory research is intended to clarify relationships of cause and effect. To that end, your design must include the means to control external or extraneous influences in order to assess hypothesized causation, usually stated as "if-then" statements. For example, you may be investigating poverty in your urban area. Implicit in explanatory research will be a cause-and-effect question: What is causing poverty in this urban area? Because you cannot take on this entire question at once, you select those aspects for intensive investigation that can help your client such as, "If federal funding declines in this urban area, then the local poverty rate will increase" or "If a major employer industry leaves the area, then the local poverty rate will increase."

Explanatory research shows the linkages between two variables and generally includes the timing (whether the cause preceded the effect), association (both variables vary together), lack of extraneous variables that might account for changes in both variables, and a reason for the relationship to exist.

What you are seeking to demonstrate is that one event has an influence on another or second event. By showing this relationship empirically, you can then develop explanations about the second event (Manheim & Rich, 1986). If we understand what affects and influences a phenomenon (the local poverty rate in the above example), then we increase our opportunities for appropriate interventions (Putt & Springer, 1989, pp. 94-95).

Useful designs that allow the testing of relationships through controlled, comparative observations are the experimental and quasi-experimental designs. Doing explanatory applied urban research requires a design that ensures unbiased and reliable observations that provide a basis for causal inferences through controlled comparisons (Cook & Campbell, 1979). Your design will provide this basis for inference if it allows you to rule out plausible, alternative explanations for the observed results. Achieving this is the topic of the next section.

RESEARCH DESIGN

The function of the research design is to organize your research project. Your design will help you integrate the specific questions, concepts, and variables into a format that allows systematic observation and analysis. The design must make sense both in terms of choosing appropriate measures for the variables and linking the research topic with urban realities. It is prudent to evaluate your design's strengths and weaknesses prior to becoming locked into the research itself. Regardless of the specifics, you can use the following checklist to help you develop your research design:

- Identify the purpose of the project
- Identify causal linkages, if appropriate
- Develop the hypotheses to be tested
- Specify your variables
- Operationalize how each variable will be measured
- Develop protocols to organize and conduct data collection and analysis
- Schedule these activities along a specified time line

This process allows you and others to understand your reasoning and operational steps. This process also provides necessary quality control and the means for receiving useful feedback. Further, the research design provides the client with the criteria for judging the validity or accuracy of your research. Just as important, a good research design will keep you on course throughout your research project.

Many times during a research project, internal and external influences can compromise your design's protocol and your eventual findings. In some cases, there are environmental factors over which you have no control (e.g., a riot's effect on police-community relations); in other cases the validity of your research hinges on the methodology's rigor (using an experimental design with *self-selected* research subjects will reduce the validity of the findings (see Boxes 4.1, 4.2, and 4.3). Trying to control for these external and internal threats before your investigation begins continues to be the primary reason for using a research design. Several design formats have been developed that offer varying degrees of control over these threats to validity.

BOX 4.1
Terms for Experimental and Quasi-Experimental Designs

The following terms are provided for your information; the language of research design can be quite esoteric, but most design references include definitions of terms. As was noted in Chapter 3, if you cannot explain your design to your client in a clear, understandable way, you may not want to use it (see Babbie, 1989, for an example of a glossary).

Dependent variable: Phenomenon that the research is interested in explaining.
Independent variable: The event or phenomenon that influences the dependent variable.
Manipulation: Intentionally creating variations in the independent variable to see the effect on the dependent variable.
Confounding variable: Extraneous or outside influences (not the independent variable) that affect the dependent variable.
Subjects: Units that are observed or tested.
Control group: The nontested group or data set with which the treatment group is compared.
Experimental (treatment) group: The group of people or data set toward which a planned change (treatment or intervention) is directed.
Randomization: The process by which subjects have an equal chance of being assigned to either the treatment group or the control group.
Internal validity: The degree to which the design provides a sound basis for inferring that the independent variable does or does not cause a change in the dependent variable. On a more applied level, it is the extent to which the phenomenon, program, or experiment rather than some other factor "caused" the effect on urban society.
External validity: The degree to which the design permits the findings to be generalized beyond the treatment group (i.e., expected to recur under similar conditions in other settings).

A quick disclaimer here: We will not completely lay out all the steps and procedures for the different types of experimental, quasi-experimental, and pre-experimental designs. Although briefly covered here, the interested reader is encouraged to consult other sources (see Babbie, 1989; Campbell & Stanley, 1966; Clark, 1979; Cook & Campbell, 1979; Hedrick et al., 1992; Lipsey, 1990; Nachmias & Nachmias, 1990).

Design Issues

Your principle task in developing a research design is to control a particular relation between variables to test for the effect of one variable on the

---

BOX 4.2
Threats to Internal Validity

Internal validity refers to the possibility that your conclusions may not accurately reflect what your design intended; that is, your conclusions are an artifact of something else. Internal validity is important in exploratory, descriptive, and explanatory research. We present the following list of threats without elaboration (see Campbell & Stanley, 1966; Cook & Campbell, 1979; Mark & Cook, 1984).

History: Events other than the intervention or treatment, occurring between your first observation and your last observation, can influence your posttest data and throw off your conclusions.

Maturation: Processes within the subjects that produce observable changes as a function of time alone, such as marriage, growth, deaths in the family, expanding population of a coastal city, and growing conservative charter of an older public organization.

Instability: Random changes and alterations in the recording of observations because of lack of communication between research team members, the researcher and the research subjects, unreliable measures, or inconsistent sampling.

Instrumentation: Using different measuring devices during the study.

Regression artifacts: This effect is seen when subjects have been selected because of extreme scores on the first test or first observation and then show improvement on the second test. However, the improvement is not the result of the independent variable or the intervention. It is a pseudoshift back toward a typical mean score ("regressing toward the mean"). This is not the result of the treatment; it simply indicates that you have selected a sample with low and unreliable scores on your first observation. They typically improve or move closer to the mean because they have nowhere to go but up and because any number of reasons may have accounted for an extraordinary event of a particularly low score.

Selection bias: Using different criteria for selecting comparison groups.

Experimental mortality: Different rates of loss of subjects from the control and treatment groups.

Selection-maturation interaction: When selection biases result in different rates of maturation that in turn contaminate the findings.

---

other (see Box 4.1). Suppose, for example, the city council in your city has decided to establish a neighborhood-improvement strategy for neighborhoods in transition. To do so, the council has funded several neighborhood associations in a pilot effort with the belief that these groups will spearhead indigenous neighborhood-improvement programs. If successful, the program will be funded citywide. The question facing the council

---

BOX 4.3
Threats to External Validity

External validity refers to the generalizability of your research findings to other settings given similar conditions (see Campbell & Stanley, 1966; Cook & Campbell, 1979; Mark & Cook, 1984). Generalizability is more important in explanatory research than in exploratory or descriptive research, where you are trying to identify accurately or clarify urban phenomena.

Interaction effects of testing: This effect occurs when your pretest (interview or observation) sensitizes the subject to the intervention or treatment to a point that it biases the posttest (i.e., the Hawthorne effect).

Interaction of selection and experimental treatment: Biased selection might produce an experimental group that is unrepresentative of the larger population, hence findings would not apply beyond this group.

Multiple-treatment interference: Simultaneous application and manipulation of several independent variables (treatments or treatment components) might interact and produce a different effect than a single treatment.

Irrelevant responsiveness of measures: Measures picking up multiple effects from the environment that have no relevance except to give the appearance of change where none has occurred.

Irrelevant replicability of treatments: If the interventions are complex, then the original researchers may not understand the actual factors that precipitated the change; future researchers or practitioners trying to replicate the program or study also will not know which components to include or which caused the change.

---

is whether this money will induce the selected neighborhood groups to take on and effectively implement neighborhood-improvement strategies such as graffiti "paint outs" and empty-lot reclamations.

The first step toward measuring whether the city council's funding of neighborhood organizations really improves the neighborhood is a consideration of design validity. Does neighborhood improvement truly reflect the effects of the independent variable (pilot funding program) or was something outside the scope of the program (such as the annual Boy Scout cleanup, which coincided with the funding of the pilot program) responsible for the effects? This is a question of ensuring internal validity—the reliability of the design.

External validity refers to the generalizability of the results to other urban settings, other urban populations, or other urban processes. Were the results generic or unique to the context and conditions of the research project? Can this particular pilot effort be expected to produce similar results in other neighborhoods? Often the enthusiasm of the researcher and the excitement surrounding a study, particularly for those being studied, create conditions that can distort actual daily routines. As another example, specially trained teachers implementing a new curriculum in inner-city schools might be more responsible for the students' elevated attention than the experimental curriculum. Under routine conditions, we cannot be sure the same results (elevated attention) would occur elsewhere. To increase the external validity (and thereby the usefulness of findings) of an applied research study of innovations in urban education, several actions can be undertaken. First, suggest trying out the new curriculum in as normal a setting as possible—in this case, training and using the regular teachers to teach the new curriculum. Also, implementing the new curriculum in a number of similar classrooms and "averaging" the results will help "wash out" any unique factors, thus providing an overall indication of the results of the new curriculum (see Weiss, 1972, p. 79). By strengthening the external validity of the research design, confidence in the exportability of the experimental curriculum is enhanced.

In both cases, the applied urban researcher must take account of a host of design threats to internal and external validity. Boxes 4.2 and 4.3 describe some of the more common validity threats. This information can be an excellent checklist for developing a research design. All research designs can be susceptible to validity threats. In effect, choosing between designs means that you are balancing your tolerance for one (or several) of many viruses or threats with the need to conduct your research. Put simply, how much uncertainty can your design tolerate? Accounting for internal validity is akin to establishing the control conditions of a laboratory experiment, where baseline data are collected on an experimental and control group before treatment is administered, and then later collecting data from both groups to assess the effects of some type of treatment or change.

Accounting for internal validity is critical to establishing causation, because the effects of influences other than the treatment are controlled. Many of the design threats noted in Box 4.2 can be lessened by using a *control group*: a group that has similar characteristics but which does not receive the treatment and is thus used for comparison. An awareness that events or activities (including how you collect data) that you did not account for can nonetheless contribute to the outcomes you are examining is a healthy way to approach design. As a rule of thumb, single-group, single-case, or static-group designs make control difficult to achieve and require additional enhancements if they are to be effective. However, single-group or single-case designs are used in evaluation research where broad knowledge of many variables is sought on one subject (e.g., agency

Table 4.1

Experimental Designs

| Subject Group | Designs | | |
	Pure Experiment	After-Only	Solomon 4-Group
Experimental	R O_1 X O_2	R X O_2	R O_1 X O_2
Control	R O_1 O_2	R O_2	R O_1 O_2
Experimental			R X O_2
Control			R O_2

or program) at a time (but see Rossi & Freeman, 1989, p. 254). The purpose of the research should drive design and, as noted above, there is no one "right" design.

In applied research we rarely can control our social setting, and yet we must settle for some information under uncertain conditions rather than none. In the next subsection we provide an overview of the ideal typical design for applied urban research: the experimental design.

Experimental Design

The experimental design is the Harley-Davidson of research designs. It is often called the *pure experiment* (i.e., pretest-posttest control group design) because it closely follows the process of natural science research. Experimental designs provide control over extraneous influences (such as accounting for the annual Boy Scout cleanup in the previous example). As Table 4.1 shows, this is achieved by the random assignment of subjects (R) into experimental and control groups, which are clearly defined independent or causal variables and dependent or affected variables, as well as by a process for pretesting (O_1) and posttesting (O_2) to ensure that the treatment (X) is actually responsible for any change in the dependent variable. *Treatment*, or *intervention*, refers to a planned effort to produce some change in a target group or area.

Thus in an experimental design we try to control for the effects of extraneous factors on a hypothesized relationship through randomization, established periods of measurement, and control groups (Welch & Comer, 1988, p. 18). Randomization allows the researcher to reduce the influence of extraneous or confounding variables because the effects would be standardized across all subjects. Randomization also avoids both intentional and unintentional bias in the selection of research subjects. Establishing periods of measurement permits the researcher to conduct a pretest to obtain baseline information and then to monitor the effects of the intervention on the research subjects (e.g., posttest). The use of a *control group*—a group of people similar in all ways to the research subjects except that they do not receive the intervention—is a final way of ascertaining cause and effect. The control group becomes a comparison group in which the effects of the intervention should not be present (O_2) given an experimental design. These characteristics provide experimental designs with strong internal validity. Several variations of the experimental design are shown in Table 4.1.

In the appropriate setting, the experimental design provides the best foundation to imply that changes in the independent variable in the research question caused the change in the dependent variable. In doing applied urban research, however, there are a variety of ethical, political, and economic reasons why it is difficult to randomly assign subjects to either a treatment group or a control group. Often programs are targeted by need, and program implementation does not conform to random selection. Consequently, the control of the laboratory is markedly reduced. For example, drug-treatment programs in urban neighborhoods often require the screening of potential clients. Waiting lists and pressure to expand treatment to underserved groups (i.e., pregnant women) make it difficult to randomly sample from the population of all potential clients.

School programs to mitigate violent gang behavior face similar problems: Random selection would necessarily qualify some schools and recreation areas for funding for new programs while others, in just as desperate straits, would be disqualified. Public outrage, unaware and unsympathetic of the need for systematic comparison, would be swift and pointed: Calls to spread the distribution of the program would be heard in council chambers. This community pressure on local elected officials, potentially alienating groups of voters, can make it difficult to conduct research using an experimental design.

These examples point to the very real problem of adapting the experimental design to meet the conditions in the urban setting. Several adaptations of the experimental design have been used with varying degrees of success, and we cover two general design categories next (see Table 4.2).

Quasi-Experimental Design

The difficulty in achieving random assignment and true control diminishes the usefulness of the experimental design in applied urban research. Quasi-experimental designs, which approximate the conditions of experimental designs, enhance the researcher's ability to make inferences about

Table 4.2
Quasi- and Pre-Experimental Designs

Subject Group	Type	Design
Nonequivalent comparison	Q	O_1 X O_2 O_1 O_2
Time series	Q	O_1 O_2 O_3 X O_4 ... O_n
One-shot case	P	X O_2
Single-group	P	O_1 X O_2
Static group	P	X O_2 O_2

the effects of an intervention on the research subjects by selecting comparable control groups, taking multiple measurements through time, or using some combination of these controls (see Cook & Campbell, 1979; Mark & Cook, 1984). The most popular quasi-experimental design is the *nonequivalent control group*, for which the researcher has not used random selection from a common population but has instead tried to find similar groups as availability permits.

A second strategy is using *multiple measurements through time* (e.g., time series). In this scenario, the researcher monitors the research subjects at several intervals to obtain pretest and posttest data. This strategy controls for the effects of confounding variables: If all of the pretest and posttest data are similar, you can be fairly certain that no external influences—outside of the intervention—have affected the research subjects. Increasing the number of observations greatly enhances internal validity and contributes to process understanding (Mark & Cook, 1984, p. 113).

The best quasi-experimental design is a combination of the nonequivalent and multiple measurement strategies. In the urban setting, these design strategies provide the necessary control for making cause-effect inferences. Constructing a quasi-experimental design requires some technical knowledge, but also calls for creativity.

Example of a Quasi-Experiment

Economic development has consistently held a top priority in urban policy making. The National Trust for Historic Preservation has contributed to this goal through its National Main Street Project, which sought to: (a) facilitate economic revitalization in central business districts (CBDs) with populations under 50,000, and (b) simultaneously preserve and promote the historical and cultural heritage of the CBDs. In short, this program was directed to small cities with CBDs of some historical import.

For cities that qualified, staff and technical assistance were provided to renovate downtown building facades, counsel merchants on advertising and marketing, and plan and conduct festivals to bring people into the CBD. Indicators of economic development in the CBD typically included such measures as the number of business start-ups, the total number of businesses, the number of renovations and new construction projects, the number of bankruptcies, the number of businesses leaving, and the number of people employed by all establishments. The Texas Main Street Project (MSP) was started in 1980, one of 27 statewide programs in the United States. By 1986, 26 small Texas cities were participating in the project. A casual observation of these cities suggested that their CBDs looked revitalized, fewer businesses were failing, new business start-ups were in evidence, and pedestrian traffic was increasing. But were these successes more apparent than real?

To explore this question, the Texas Historical Commission requested an assessment of the gains made by the MSP. A research design was developed to assess the effects of the MSP in all 26 participating cities, compare MSP cities with a nonequivalent control group of similarly sized cities, and then assess changes in sales revenues and employment in both groups of cities during the period of the MSP, 1980-1986 (see Riposa & Slack, 1986). The study was to be completed in 180 days and the funding was limited (e.g., limited travel, no funds were provided to assist cities in collecting and providing data). (However, MSP cities were required to submit data on a variety of conditions in their CBDs as part of their initial application in 1980.)

It was easy enough to randomly select a number of small Texas cities manifesting similar characteristics to the MSP cities. It turned out that there was no way to collect archival data in the control cities, however (staff were unavailable to collect archival data), making a pretest comparison difficult. Consequently, the study relied on an analysis of pretest-posttest data from the MSP cities to discover what effect the MSP had in those cities' CBDs, and it compared 1986 data on the economic development indicators from both groups, which was accessible and comparable, to see how the MSP cities fared in achieving economic development gains in their CBDs compared with other cities. The final part of the analysis (comparing sales revenues and employment in both groups of cities for the period 1980-1986), lacking comparable pretest data, was conducted, but the results were inconclusive.

As it turned out, the study found that the MSP did have a direct positive effect on CBD revitalization, and it identified several additional factors that might affect the success of the MSP, including proximity to transportation routes, proximity to major urban centers, the characteristics of MSP managers, and existing patterns of public-private cooperation.

Pre-Experimental Designs

Some designs lack pretests or other forms of control, thus contributing to problems of internal and external validity. These are the single-group pretest-posttest, single-case study, and static-group comparison designs. Pre-experimental designs lack power to make inferences because of the nagging possibility that unaccounted-for confounding variables have affected the dependent variable.

The single-case study does not assess the condition of the subject prior to the treatment; without a baseline, it is hard to measure change. Research using this design often compares outcomes against a given norm such as a national average, statewide average, or some other similar aggregate measure. Even so, without accounting for the effects of extraneous influences, it is difficult to know whether the outcome can indeed be attributed to the treatment. Research on gangs tends to show that gang affiliation decreases with age. Gang-mitigation programs targeting urban teenagers (e.g., skills training and counseling) that fail to pretest cannot determine effectiveness without knowing whether the "successes" (those who dropped their gang affiliation) stemmed from the program of individual growth and development.

The single-group pretest posttest design has the capability of showing association between treatment and outcome; however, the lack of a control group in this design does not permit us to determine whether the treatment made any difference. Often this design incorporates comparison with a national or other standard (e.g., standardized test scores in education). Finally, the results of a static-group comparison design depend on how similar the two groups were before treatment; without pretesting in a diverse urban environment, equivalence may prove to be a faulty assumption and call into question the eventual research findings.

In spite of their weak claims of validity, these designs can partially describe in a limited time what is happening in a particular situation, thereby permitting a preliminary assessment of association between variables. Although lacking in control, pre-experimental designs can be useful to get a quick fix on an issue or to suggest directions for future research. We would always recommend using a more rigorous design; however, in a crunch, you sometimes have to work with what you have at your disposal, understanding that there are limitations in your findings. Recognizing these limits in advance and creatively devising coping strategies is part of the process of developing the research design.

ADMINISTERING APPLIED URBAN RESEARCH THROUGH THE DESIGN

In addition to providing a method for systematically implementing your research project, the research design provides you with a research-management tool. Applied urban research, with its collaborative, problem-solving orientation, requires that certain activities occur regardless of the type of design that you use. In this section we identify the steps necessary to ensure that your design helps you keep your research on course.

After selecting the design, you must translate it into operational terms. To do this means identifying and describing the tasks that will be needed to implement the design. Each task will then require a description of how it contributes to the project, the task-specific resource needs (e.g., staff, cost), and the time needed for task completion. The goal is to complete the project on time; this means that you need to establish a buffer at the end of the project so that you can have a draft copy of your findings or report reviewed and cleaned up before final submission.

If your research project is being conducted with others, then team roles need to be specified and responsibilities made clear. In addition, if you are doing a team project, all team members should be present and involved in the operationalization of the design; if you have support staff (e.g., graphics, secretarial, and statistical) it is a good idea to include them early in the process, too. Establishing a team requires team building, and role-clarification activities can help achieve this end.

Team building should include progress and feedback meetings for the staff responsible for that task; if you are doing the project on your own, set up meetings (these can be telephone meetings to which you FAX necessary documents beforehand) with your client at critical points throughout the project (e.g., design selection, data collection, and reporting). One of the purposes for these meetings is to reduce the risk of unpleasant surprises or new developments as the project nears its deadline.

Like your ideal research design, project planning should be rigorous: Plan for all contingencies before everyone starts pulling out calendars and discussing specific days and times of meetings. It is a good idea to have a ballpark estimate of the effort needed for the most rigorous design (i.e., experimental) so that the research project can be successfully completed within time and budget constraints. Hedrick et al. (1992) discuss these issues in greater detail.

SUMMARY

This chapter provided an overview of the research design process by linking design with the function or purpose of your applied urban research. Three research purposes were discussed—exploration, description, and explanation—and design capabilities were discussed in relation to each. In terms of research design, we summarized experimental, quasi-experimental, and pre-experimental designs around the theme of design validity. Applied urban research is susceptible to certain validity threats, and several strategies were noted to help overcome the most common threats. We closed the chapter by suggesting that your research design also can be a useful administrative tool.

EXERCISE

By this time, your team has developed some familiarity with a particular urban issue. Now it is time to develop your strategy to investigate this issue or problem on which your team has focused in previous weeks. Begin by reviewing the questions that help you, the researcher, select your eventual design. What are the questions that present your group with the most difficulty at this point? How will you deal with these? What design issues does your project need to address? Now select a design format and note the justifications for selecting this particular design. How are you going to deal with the limitations of your design; are they of any consequence to your project? Does your approach or level of analysis influence your decision? (You may need to go to the library and read some portions of the background sources we have provided in this section.) Members of the group will need to bring their background research to the team meeting and contribute to the drafting and diagraming of your design, which will be presented in class, submitted to the instructor, or both.

5

Data Collection in the Urban Setting

DATA SOURCES AND RESOURCES

Data collection can either be a straightforward task or require the knack of Sherlock Holmes for unraveling a mystery from the smallest clue. Either way, your familiarity with the availability and accessibility of urban data sources and resources, as well as your creativity in discovering and mining "new" data sources, can prove to be the critical link in the research chain. Although researchers with different disciplinary backgrounds might prefer to use the data collection methods favored by their disciplines, it is important to remember that different methods can be equally useful when applied correctly.

In this chapter we provide an overview of the two general categories of data collection methods: primary and secondary methods. Primary data collection is the responsibility of the researcher. You are responsible for designing, collecting, and summarizing the data. You need to identify the questions that are to be asked, design measurement instruments (e.g., questionnaires and data summary sheets), and identify respondents (see Fetterman, 1989; Fowler, 1988; Harrison, 1987; Yin, 1989; all are in this series). Secondary data are those that have already been collected and summarized, generally for purposes other than your research project. Using secondary data still requires identifying research questions, identifying and evaluating existing data sources, and designing ways to use the secondary data to address your research questions (see Cooper, 1989; Rosenthal, 1984; Stewart, 1984; all in this series). Often, primary and secondary data are used to complement each other. Our presentation in this chapter is intended to be broad and urban-focused in scope; greater depth may be found by consulting the works cited above or in each section. The first section of the chapter discusses secondary data sources; the second section discusses primary data sources. Each section provides general checklists for data collection. Describing and accessing these sources are the themes of this chapter.

Before you begin to explore the data that may be available, you should first be very clear: Why are you collecting data? Ideally, you will have decided this as well as what type of data to obtain during the strategic-thinking and research-design processes. How to reconcile other needs with data collection was a topic for research design (other needs might include ensuring the validity of the data, identifying the units and level of analysis of your research project, meeting its time frame and perhaps budget, and complementing and expanding your knowledge of data sources).

Regardless of the data collection method used, you should first consider the likely topics, formats, and sources of information. Where might data be available and easily accessed? What level of detail would you like to achieve? Each question should lead you to consider a variety of sources and resources.

SECTION 1: SECONDARY DATA

This section reviews documentary and archival sources of data and their usefulness for various types of urban research projects (see Murphy, 1980; Salant, 1990). Secondary data are useful at all levels of analysis. This section begins with a review of data sources from the national, state, and local levels of government that focus on or provide important information for urban research. Next, harder-to-find or fugitive sources are discussed. This section concludes with a checklist for using secondary data sources.

Source Questions in Collecting Data

What constitutes data? Data sources include persons, places, things, events, and outcomes (see Box 5.1). Data can come from process (e.g., policy making or community involvement) or substance (e.g., housing, education, or crime). In short, anything and everything can be considered as a source for data. Because of the vast array of available and fairly accessible published and unpublished data, it is easy to feel swamped. If you have a clear sense of *why* you need data (that is, a good theoretical formulation of the problem and research design), you can more easily chart a course through the many data sources and resources that are available. You might find that using secondary sources fits the bill; in many cases, secondary data may be sufficient for your research needs. In other cases, you might discover that there are no data sources or resources that meet your needs or that existing sources do not provide the angle your research project requires. Often this is true of exploratory research. In such cases, you need to select a data collection strategy that can be completed within

---

BOX 5.1
What Are Data?

Data come in a variety of ways, manifesting a variety of characteristics of persons, places, events, and outcomes. The following briefly lists possible variables in each category.

Persons: age, sex, gender, ethnicity, education, employment status, social status, religion, and income

Places: urban, rural, size of city, MSA, population, size of neighborhood, type of residence, precinct voting registration, and voter turnout

Events: election results, earthquake damage, and types and frequency of protests

Outcomes: poverty rates, budget expenditures, levels of affordable housing, high school matriculation rates, crime rates, unemployment rates, size of the underclass, tax rates, and damages from inner-city urban rebellions

---

the constraints of your project's time frame and budget and which conforms to your research design.

Because it is very difficult to catalog all of the data sources that are available or to find "fugitive" data resources (those that are not generally released and which are harder to find, such as the Texas MSP study referenced in the previous chapter), when you are working under a time constraint, it is useful to know where you can get your hands on data sources and resources. For example, knowing which libraries serve as government repositories, how complete your library's holdings are, and the major resources in your field that have urban-oriented sources (e.g., *United States Political Science Documents* and *Sage Urban Abstracts* in our field of political science) are good starting questions. Knowing that most of these indexes also conveniently provide key words can help get you moving. Finally, it is useful to have a couple of backup strategies in mind, such as quick reference sources (a colleague or reference librarian) who can answer your data questions in a knowledgeable way about what data are available and easily accessible. Begin by acquainting yourself with the local university or public library, from the reference librarian to the on-line catalog system. This is the first step in accessing general urban information and data sources and resources.

Resources Available for Urban Research

A wealth of sources are available locally that can provide data useful to your research. Local general purpose (city and county), metropolitan (councils of government and special districts), and special purpose (school, water and sewer, and transit) governments are big data users and often good sources of information; much of the data used by officials in these agencies are collected by the federal government, but locally generated special reports often provide information of special interest (usually through specialized computer programs or localized surveys or focus groups) that is not readily available elsewhere. Do not overlook the usefulness of government telephone directories as a source of information; although local public officials are busy people, you can often get specific questions answered over the telephone.

In addition to local governments, nonprofit organizations may have data resources. Church-sponsored social organizations may collect data on numbers of persons using shelters or other services; community organizations may have conducted neighborhood or community surveys on important issues in the neighborhood (e.g., crime and police protection, education, economic opportunity, and quality of neighborhood life); and local and area foundations may have community, citywide, regional, or national data resources. Professional associations (organized by function) are another excellent source of information, and these organizations produce directories that are as useful as government telephone directories.

You should consider commercially produced data sources such as those produced by your local chamber of commerce. Also do not overlook your local newspapers, particularly the local alternative city paper (e.g., the *Reader* or *Weekly*), which can provide excellent, if underutilized, contextual data sources (e.g., through controversies, exposes, and counteropinions) for exploring issues of local interest from the local perspective. In addition, these data sources can help you identify other resources (names of persons or organizations for follow-up), suggest data collection methods, and help determine the ease or difficulty of conducting your research project.

Federal Sources

Published urban-oriented data resources collected by the federal government include all of the big agencies in the federal statistical system: the Department of Housing and Urban Development (HUD), the Bureau of the Census, the Centers for Disease Control and Prevention, the Bureau of Justice Statistics, the Bureau of Labor Statistics, the Bureau of Economic Analysis, the National Center of Health Statistics, the Center for

Table 5.1

Finding Federal Data for Urban Research

Agency (Department)	Type of Data
Housing and Urban Development	Housing activities including urban development public housing; finances; occupancy and vacancy; projects, communities, and people assisted (e.g., rental loan data); Community Development Block Grant data
Bureau of the Census (Commerce)	Population, housing, manufacturing, current economic indicators (retail and wholesale trade), state and local government finances, and employment
Bureau of Justice Statistics (Justice)	Crime and victimization, justice expenditures, employment
Bureau of Labor Statistics (Labor)	Labor economics: employment, manpower, wages, productivity and technology developments, industrial relations, work injuries, prices and costs, standard of living
Bureau of Economic Analysis (Commerce)	Local personal income, current business statistics, investment (including direct foreign investment)
Centers for Disease Control and Prevention (Health and Human Services)	Public health: epidemiology, environmental health, state and local health departments, occupational safety and health
Energy Information Administration	Long-term energy trends, macroeconomic impacts of energy trends in regions; energy resources, production, demand, consumption, and distribution

Statistics (formerly the National Center for Education Statistics), the Statistical Reporting Service, and the Energy Information Administration. These agencies collect data to meet mission and program needs (several are profiled in Table 5.1).

On a continuing basis, the federal agencies provide a variety of different categories of data describing different aspects and facets of urban life. Two very useful general sources are the annual *U.S. Government Manual* produced by the Government Printing Office in Washington, D.C., and the *Guide to U.S. Government Statistics* (Androit, Androit, & Androit, 1986). HUD has a multiple-volume listing (the *Dictionary Catalog of the U.S. Department of Housing and Urban Development*) of all materials in the agency's national office in Washington, D.C. You also can access HUD resources through HUD USER, an on-line computer service.

Currently, the first data from the Bureau of the Census's 1990 population census are being made available; the timetable for release of the 1990 data continues into 1993. Census data can be accessed through reports, microfiche, the on-line CENDATA system, and on CD-ROM (i.e., compact-disc files). The Census Bureau provides a variety of free publications that describe the content of the agency's data, such as *Census ABC's, Census '90 Basics, Two Hundred Years and Counting, The 1990 Census*, and the *Tabulation and Publication Program*. Census data can be found in the government documents sections of public (government repository) libraries.

Census data are a major source of information for doing applied urban research. The uniformity and consistency of the data, coupled with the breakdown of census data to the block level, provide urban researchers a comprehensive and reliable data base. The Bureau of the Census also publishes statistics on local governments (e.g., comparative data on finances, functions, and governmental fragmentation, among other categories) in the *Census of Governments* and *The County and City Data Book*. Two other useful sources are the *Statistical Abstract of the United States* and the *State and Metropolitan Area Data Book*. If you would like to explore some of the uses of census data in applied research, we recommend *Census ABC's* as an excellent starting resource. If this publication is not available at your local library, call the bureau's Data User Services Division (301-763-4100) for assistance.

Using federal data, however, requires caution. Census data are usually —but not always—comparable across states (although the 1990 data differ from the 1980 data because several collection categories have been changed, the most notable being that enumeration districts are no longer used and the entire nation is now "blocked"—that is, data are collected at the block level). Two other well-rehearsed examples are criminal-justice and unemployment data. Although the Bureau of Justice Statistics provides a wide range of criminal-justice information (see the *Sourcebook of Criminal Justice Statistics* or the *Report to the Nation on Crime and Justice*), this information is grounded in state criminal-justice policies. Why is this important? First-time users who may not be aware of state-by-state differences in definitions, prison terms, sentencing, and "good behavior" parole requirements will be dismayed at the ensuing difficulty in comparing probation and parole statistics across states. Unemployment insurance data are also hard to compare between states (and over time) because of differences in eligibility requirements and the extent to which workers are covered by state insurance programs. Therefore, users should still be sure to determine comparability!

State and Local Government Sources

At the state level, you can find data sources and resources either in the legislature (most states have a local government committee that deals with governance issues and is a useful place to start your inquiry) or in the executive branch agency responsible for the urban policy issue you are researching. Or start at the state budget office, which is listed in the blue pages of your telephone directory. In addition to responding to data or information questions, committee staff or agency officials also can help you identify other data sources (make sure that you *always* ask for the document identification number for reports, regulations, or laws). If you are unclear about which agency conducts what program, consult your directory of state agencies, which is available in your library.

In the largest cities, data needs are addressed by departmental staff. Good places to start are in the city clerk's, city manager's, or city administrator's office or in the department responsible for policy in the issue area of your research. In the city manager's office, identify the administrative assistant responsible for policy in the area of your research and deal directly with this person. When inquiring at city departments, telephone the department head's office directly (remember to have specific questions ready). Box 5.2 illustrates a typical data summary sheet that can be used when contacting public officials.

Most state and local agencies produce a variety of decision-making aids for internal or external consumption (e.g., memoranda; calendars; electronic mail; proceedings, reports, and evaluations; background or briefing papers; and presentations to other agencies, especially at the regional level). These documents often contain good information, such as summaries of policies and policy alternatives, and provide the names of potential information sources for follow-up. An excellent example of using locally generated data (on taxes, indebtedness, and elections) in urban analysis can be seen in Erie (1992).

Also available from agencies are organizational and budgetary information, documents that are critical for applied research that is examining urban service delivery or policy management. These documents are generally available, but you will have to go to the agency to gain access. In some cases, data and codebooks describing and explaining the data (making the data accessible) are not kept together, so be sure to inquire about availability ahead of time. In addition to providing source material, these documents provide an illustration of how to report your research back to policy makers. If you are going in "cold" (without a contact), the agency's public information office can help you get started.

BOX 5.2
Contacting Public Officials

Preparing a data summary or interview protocol that you can use when contacting public officials is a good way to quickly find out where to get data. Always ask if you can call back with clarifying questions in the future.

Name: Phone Number:
Date:

Introduction and Question

Agency	Type of Contact	Name	Phone Number

Documents

Reports (Name)	(Report Number)	(Send?)

Other

Can I call you back if I have additional questions?   Y   N

Public meetings are another good source of data once you have identified a decision-making process. These not only provide an unobtrusive data gathering opportunity, but also make agendas, minutes, and other forms of documentation available. In many metropolitan areas, citizen's advisory boards operate through public meetings, providing you with additional data sources (city governments have directories of these groups). This combination of data gathering opportunities helps build accuracy and confidence in your findings.

Regional councils of government (COGs) provide another data source and perspective on urban issues, particularly those issues that cut across jurisdictional lines (such as the so-called quality-of-life issues of the environment, health, economic development, homelessness, and education). Most COGs have a research division that uses some combination of demographers, statisticians, geographers, economists, and others who regularly provide information to planning and other departments. COGs have bulletins or indexes that list all of the reports and often contain abstracts that are a useful quick reference. In addition, COGs usually use geographic information systems to provide maps for use in facilities planning (location decisions), hospitals (market area detail), transit operators (journey to work), and the private sector (market analysis). Excellent maps are generally available at little or no cost.

Professional Associations

Professional associations are an excellent urban research resource. Professional associations represent their members' interests and serve as an information network for members; as such, associations are clearinghouses for certain types of information. Most of the larger national associations (e.g., the American Planning Association and the American Society for Public Administration) have regional chapters or groups located in the major metropolitan areas across the United States. These associations or their regional chapters can provide you with local or regional contacts as well as data.

One of the most useful general urban information resources is published by the International City-County Management Association (ICMA), the annual *Municipal Year Book*. This resource includes a "Sources of Information" appendix that references a variety of sources across 15 functional headings (e.g., emergency management, public finances, and personnel) and includes both hard data sources and on-line sources. In addition, narrative summaries based on data obtained through ICMA member surveys provide a somewhat unique perspective on current issues in urban areas throughout the United States.

A multivolume guide to professional associations, the *Directory of Professional Associations*, is published by Gale Directories and is available through most public or university libraries. Most occupational groups have formed professional associations, and these will be listed in this directory.

Nonprofit Organizations

A variety of nonprofit organizations provide another urban research resource. Area foundations (e.g., Ford, W. K. Kellogg, John D. and Katherine T. MacArthur, and McKnight), academically oriented groups (e.g., the Social Science Research Council), and other institutions collect information relevant to their program areas. These institutions are an excellent source of information on neighborhood and citywide issues. For example, the League of Women Voters has an annual publication titled "Urban Briefs," which is an annotated series on government documents and academic literature sources. Other nonprofit organizations can be found in the *Foundation Directory*.

Commercial Sources

Urban areas are also served by a variety of commercial data and information sources (see Stewart, 1984). Two generally useful resources are chambers of commerce and daily newspapers. A chamber of commerce is the pulse of the business community and should be regarded as a prime information resource. Chambers produce community data books and other materials that are used to market the city (e.g., infrastructure, employment, education, and workforce characteristics); these are good reference materials for both what is shown and what is absent in the presentations. Chamber functions, not all of which are open to the general public, may also provide opportunities to "get to know" business leaders. Depending on the city you are in, other business and commercial data may be available to the public on a limited basis (e.g., real estate boards, business councils, and public-private enterprises).

Most libraries have indexes for the largest daily newspapers (e.g., *The New York Times*). Newspapers themselves keep paper or electronic archives of most of their articles and stories. Contacting reporters can provide you with access to these files and may even provide leads to other sources. Your city's alternative newspaper also can provide an interesting counterpoint to the standard news fare.

Academic Sources

A variety of academically oriented research resources are available for your use. In addition to discipline-based indexes and abstracts, the *Social Science Index* (SSI) and the *Public Affairs Index Service* (PAIS) provide general listings of scholarly articles, magazine articles, books, and government documents (see Stewart, 1984). Several academic presses have monograph series that are dedicated to the examination of urban issues (e.g., the University of Kansas Press and the State University of New York Press).

Some universities have urban affairs programs that usually include a research unit. Table 5.2 lists some university-based urban programs. These units conduct research at all levels of analysis and can be helpful to your research project. One current data collection effort that is focused on developing a comparative database is the Fiscal Austerity and Urban Innovation (FAUI) Project, which began in 1982 (a 36-country database is being compiled). Data are available through the Inter-University Consortium for Social and Political Research (see I-UCSPR, 1988) at Ann Arbor, Michigan, and a newsletter is available (see Clark, 1990; Clarke, 1990).

Table 5.2
Selected University-Based Urban Studies Programs

State	University
Alabama	Alabama A&M
California	San Diego State; UCLA; UC Berkeley; San Francisco State
Connecticut	Southern Connecticut
Delaware	U. of Delaware
District of Columbia	U. of District of Columbia
Georgia	Georgia State
Illinois	Northeastern; U. of Chicago
Kentucky	U. of Louisville
Louisiana	U. of New Orleans
Maryland	U. of Maryland
Massachusetts	Boston U.; Tufts; MIT
Michigan	Michigan State
Minnesota	Mankato State
New Jersey	Montclair State
New York	Hunter; Long Island U.; New School; Queens; Rensselaer; Syracuse
Ohio	Akron; Cleveland State; Wright State
Oregon	Portland State
Pennsylvania	Carnegie Mellon; Temple
Texas	U. of Texas, Arlington; Trinity
Virginia	Old Dominion
Wisconsin	U. of Wisconsin—Milwaukee

Using Different Secondary Sources and Methods

The issue of data collection is closely bound with the substantive and design concerns of your research project, as well as by your knowledge of what types of data may be available. Our contention is that you should collect as much data as possible, scanning and filtering them against the guidelines of your research question, a set time period, and the other needs of your project (e.g., costs).

No rule precludes you from using more than one technique to generate several different data sets to address your research problem; indeed, this increasingly seems to be common practice (Brewer & Hunter, 1989). Furthermore, such an approach can enhance the validity of your findings (through the triangulation of several data sources) or may set up the examination of an issue through primary methods (e.g., doing fieldwork at the neighborhood level or a citywide survey).

A general caveat to the use of secondary data: Before using secondary information sources, you must ascertain their quality and reliability. Is the information accurate and will it really do what your research requires? Stewart (1984, pp. 23-32) addresses this concern by asking six questions:

1. What was the purpose of the original collection?
2. Who collected the information?
3. What information was actually collected?
4. When was the information collected?
5. How was the information collected?
6. How consistent is the information with other sources?

Only in knowing the context of secondary sources can you be sure of their reliability.

SECTION 2: PRIMARY DATA

One of the main tasks of primary data collection is collecting information not available elsewhere. Primary data can be collected at all levels of analysis, but the potentially high costs associated with their collection increase at levels beyond the regional level (i.e., national and world systems of cities). Strategies for primary collection, such as the FAUI Project noted above, have to cope with these costs. In an applied urban investigation, one of your main data sources will be people. Your predominant source will likely be local public officials, but you will also draw from different constituency groups, depending on the research topic and level of analysis. Access to these groups will vary.

In this section, the focus is on primary research or research that will elicit some response through interviews. We begin by suggesting starting points to gain access to relevant actors and then take up unobtrusive and face-to-face interviewing in the field. Next we provide an overview of urban survey data collection. Checklists are provided to help you in your work.

A General Map of Urban Sources

In this section, we assume that you have decided that your research project demands some form of personal response to provide insight into your research question. This prospect is warranted in many cases, particularly if attitudes and behavior are the focus of your research question. A variety of field research techniques, including direct interviewing, field observation, and mail surveys allow you to tap attitudes and behaviors. Because so much applied urban research deals with public policy, we have provided a brief inventory of policy actors (see Herson & Bolland, 1990, pp. 201-210).

Formal Actors

The following institutions and actors are the most visible participants in the policy adoption and implementation process. Through their decisions, urban space is produced in all of its forms.

Mayor: Strong mayors have the power to hire and fire key personnel and, just as important, work with the chief administrative officer (CAO) in preparing the budget for the city council. Usually, the strong mayor is a full-time position, providing access to the media, important community groups, and the city council. This increases the mayor's influence over setting the urban agenda.

City council: Legislative body, elected at-large or by district (or ward), that typically selects the city manager, votes on the city budget, and influences the allocation of federal funds and mayoral appointments to boards and commissions.

Administrators: These public servants are the interpreters and implementors of policy. Their power and influence become pivotal as they draw upon technical expertise, control over information, and their monopoly over implementation.

Street-level bureaucrats: These are the employees of city bureaucracies who implement public policy with a great degree of discretion (e.g., police officers, teachers, clerks, planning technicians, inspectors, and public health and welfare workers).

Community advisory boards and commissions: Usually appointed, these citizen committees make nonbinding recommendations to the city administration.

Informal Actors

These actors generate the demands and supports directed at governing institutions throughout the policy process.

Clients: Citizens who are the recipients of and rely on certain publicly provided services.

Voters: Citizens casting preferences that indicate participation patterns and public priorities.

Protesters: Violent and nonviolent protests draw attention to emerging salient issues and potentially powerful groups not addressed in the policy process.

Neighborhood associations: These groups are integral in quality-of-life and tax issues (homeowners' associations).

Economic interests: The business community, represented individually or by associations, plays a pivotal role in development policy, which is a central topic on the urban agenda. As a result, city officials bring economic elites into the inner circle of decision making.

Now that you have a general idea about the available primary resources, we can discuss primary data collection methods.

In the Field and Face-to-Face

Field research holds a special status. In applied urban research we often must leave the safety of our academic or institutional surroundings and venture into a new and often unfamiliar environment that may resist casual viewing and entry. Educational credentials or professional position might not carry you in this environment. For instance, if you are conducting interviews with city officials, your credentials might be useful in gaining access. The same is not true if you are observing and interviewing urban street gang members in their "hood" (see Horowitz, 1983; Riposa & Dersch, 1990).

In applied urban research, field data collection poses a paradox. Urban field sites are both familiar and foreign (Posner, 1980, p. 205). Consequently, the researcher inevitably switches back and forth between urban cultures, going from home to office to field site, often in the same day. Without proper planning and the proper mindset, the office-field transition can result in a loss of objectivity that can jeopardize your research project.

To get started, you will have to make a decision about your method (i.e., are you an observer, participant-observer, or participant?), what and who you will observe, and who you will interview (see Fetterman, 1989; Nachmias & Nachmias, 1990). Conducting an effective field program demands that you allot time for planning, entry, observation, and interviews, if required.

Getting Started

One recurrent theme of this book is strategic thinking. Doing fieldwork to collect data requires the same attention to strategy as does developing your research design. The following points will help you plan for an effective field data collection experience (see Jorgensen, 1989, pp. 29-36; Schatzman & Strauss, 1973, p. 18; Spector, 1980, p. 100).

- Use secondary data to provide a useful context for clues:
  conduct literature reviews on your research site
  use directories and local resource people to develop your fieldwork
    itinerary
- Be flexible when in the field—stand back, observe, and record—patterns
  will emerge
- Use multiple indicators to increase your validity
- Case various sites to conduct your interviews, using the criteria of suitability
  (substance) and feasibility (size of target population, cost, and cultural
  barriers)
- Construct a social map of the players according to spheres of influence, danger
  zones (sensitive areas), liaison people, resources, and gatekeepers
- Schedule your interviewing and observing time to allow the organization of
  your data

One useful casing technique is the *windshield survey*. Its purpose usually is to assess your research topic or area. As the name suggests, driving (or walking at a neighborhood level) through your areas of interest is a good way to become familiar with the context of your research. It is a good idea to prepare a checklist to help orient your observations. For example, if you are researching historic preservation in the downtown, which is a common feature of economic development, your checklist might include the condition of sidewalks, streetlights, the number of adult enterprises, the number of boarded or otherwise unused buildings, as well as the condition of older buildings (e.g., two to three stories in height, common brick, continuous facades at the property line, cornices separating the ground floor from the upper floors, and window design are common architectural elements to be noted in historic districts). The checklist should be developed based on your data needs. The role of observer should be kept distinct from the role of driver.

Having done this, you can select a method for sampling. If you are going to interview a group that fits a clearly defined category of participants, you could rely on the *quota method* (a nonprobability sample in which respondents are selected based on prespecified characteristics assumed to exist in the target population; see Babbie, 1989, p. 268). But if you have limited knowledge and few scheduled interviews, then asking your respondents for additional names allows you to "snowball" your interview itinerary. To study the gap between atypical and typical urban behavior, you might want to interview people who manifest deviant behavior. Finally, if you have a good grasp of your area of inquiry, you can select your interviewees based on their knowledge and experience. This is known as using a purposive itinerary.

Studying What Is in Front of Your Nose

Applied urban research often requires gaining firsthand knowledge about the research subject, which means doing fieldwork. Participant observation is basic to fieldwork (see Fetterman, 1989). This method of data collection refers to the researcher taking an active role in the research site, often in close contact with the research subjects (i.e., people at the site). Suppose the city parks and recreation department has asked you to observe how youths use public places for the department's activities-planning process. You could study how young adults use parking lots after school to help the department develop public parks programs that would attract rather than repel teenage users. Therefore, you have decided to study how teenagers use parking lots so that the department can duplicate this atmosphere in its park system. To effectively use observation as a method of data collection, however, you first have to know the "rules of the game."

Public places are guided by social norms or assumptions of expected behavior (Karp, 1980). So when you enter public places for observation, you must be aware that locals may act as gatekeepers who give or deny access. For example, in research on violent urban street gangs, it was necessary to observe gang members in their territorially claimed park areas. Observing how gang members interacted with one another and with outsiders (e.g., civilians, other gang members, and police) provided clues on the norms of introduction and which key leaders served as gatekeepers to the park (Riposa & Dersch, 1990). A strategy for doing this type of data collection includes the following steps (Box 5.3 discusses a typical data collection experience).

1. Take notes unobtrusively, and only a key note or two if you must. It is preferable to record your experiences in your field journal after you leave the research site.
2. Wear clothing that blends into the research site.
3. Use proper introductions when necessary. At times, you will need to have formal or prearranged meetings with gatekeepers.
4. Casual conversations that are not interviews can be used for data collection.
5. Let your feelings help interpret your observations; trust your intuition.
6. Use multiple indicators for quality control.

Strategies for Getting Interviews

One-on-One. Interviews are a way to gain and maintain access to the activities, experiences, and beliefs of the research subjects (Hoffman,

---

BOX 5.3
Collecting Data on the Street

At first, doing applied research on violent urban street gangs to suggest policies that might reduce joining and violent behavior seemed to defy convention. Of course, the field and research area demanded flexibility. The following steps describe the data collection process (Riposa & Dersch, 1990).

Literature review: We read both scholarly and popular accounts of urban gangs to develop a context and a sense of the changes that street gangs manifested.

Theorizing: After the review, we developed a theory that gang policies were ineffective because local agencies had not taken into account the changes in gangs over the last 20 years.

Field protocol: We then developed our plan to observe gangs in the field and how we would eventually conduct our interviews.

Unobtrusive observation: Living in gang neighborhoods allowed us some daily observation; to increase our observations, we visited and hung out at the local parks and fast food places controlled by different gangs. Because our dress and demeanor fit the local neighborhood culture, we blended in and went unnoticed.

Entry: We were introduced to other gang members by those members we had met through the Social Services Department and at university programs or who had become familiar with us in the neighborhood. The police arranged some interviews on the street and defense attorneys arranged interviews for us with gang members awaiting trial.

Interviews: We then conducted face-to-face, open-ended field interviews with members of African-American, Latino, and Asian gangs.

The entire process—from initiation until we presented our findings at a professional conference—took approximately 11 months.

1980, p. 45). At a minimum, you will want to interview key players or people directly involved in the activities under examination. Of course, obstacles exist. Cultural differences can make potential participants hesitant, key actors might see you as a threat, or your research project might not be organized enough that your information needs are clear to the respondent. To overcome these and other problems, follow a few simple tips.

First, case the site and see what type of entry obstacles exist. Will you need a translator? Will you need a local community person to introduce you around to allay fears? Who are the people you will want for initial interviews? To examine the political incorporation of the Cambodian population in Long Beach, California, the largest concentration of this ethnic group in the United States, introductions, translators, and permission for interviews were essential (Riposa, 1991).

Second, be accurate and be honest, but be brief. Present your project in a pointed, succinct way; even a willing interviewee will give you only a limited amount of time, so be clear and to the point. Sometimes a letter in advance is useful; again keep it short (no more than one page).

Third, be sensitive to personal and institutional privacy—at least initially. Tapping the appropriate vein of information demands that you understand the process in which you are involved. Many people are hesitant at first to be studied. They might be shy, might not want to be bothered, might not believe it serves any useful purpose, or might have something to hide. As Goffman (1967) asks, how can researchers overcome the "front work," those superficial public versions of what the institution or key individual is about? To overcome the "front" that each of us erects for protection, you need to be subtle and sensitive. Here are some additional techniques upon which to draw (Hoffman, 1980, pp. 47-52):

- Dress appropriately for the research site—consider the locals when you dress
- Familiarize yourself with your interview protocol—develop the appropriate secondary probes in advance
- Use social ties and friendships to breech difficult access points and establish trust with the respondent
- Use deflection to overcome closed doors or defensiveness—bury the central question in your introductory remarks or a question about some external situation or individual
- Keep a poker face

Strengths and Weaknesses. Field research is best for studying nuances and attitudes and for examining social processes over time (Babbie, 1989, p. 285). Some of the foci of field data collection are roles, relationships, encounters, hidden meanings, and practices (Lofland, 1984). Going face-to-face provides the opportunity to take advantage of serendipitous points as they emerge. Field data collection also provides flexibility and allows the researcher to experience the field context and thereby gain depth in understanding. Often we are unable to construct a questionnaire that allows us to penetrate the conditions and nuances of our research site. For example, when querying drug addicts in the mission district of your city about their perceptions of the accessibility to treatment programs, it is imperative to observe and talk to the people directly in a language they understand. Such situations are less amenable to the use of a mailed questionnaire or phone survey.

Weaknesses in the approach also are evident. Interpretation can suffer from the threat to precise information: You can misinterpret the interview responses or ask the wrong question. Difficulty in replication may result because later researchers may not be able to reconstruct the atmosphere and conditions of your original interview. Being comprehensive and systematic can help diminish these possibilities.

Survey Data Collection

Suppose you want to examine several characteristics of a large population. Face-to-face interviewing would neither be feasible nor provide you with the variety of responses needed for generalization. At this juncture you need to consider survey data collection. In this section, we will discuss some of the essentials for doing urban survey data collection in applied urban research. Our goal is to get the urban researcher started and alert the investigator to the pitfalls that can inhibit systematic survey data collection. We make no pretense to review the survey methodology, except to say that surveys are generally direct, self-administered by mail, or conducted by telephone. Each requires its own design and has its own strengths and weaknesses (see Dillman, 1978; also Fowler, 1988, in this series).

However, before embarking on a survey, consider whether you really need to collect information in this way. As Fowler (1988, p. 11) notes, surveys are an expensive way to collect information and should only be undertaken if the need for the information is significant or the data on a population cannot be collected in another way (e.g., from existing records). Or you may need to collect large-scale data that do not already exist (e.g., community surveys focusing on growth management or other recent urban initiatives).

Sample Frame. The critical feature of survey data collection lies in the accuracy of designing a sample frame (see Fowler, 1988). In some cases, the client can provide a list of the target population from which you can devise your sample frame. If the client cannot provide such a list, you can obtain lists of potential respondents from precinct (election) lists, professional association directories, community organization membership or attendance roles, or constituents of school or other special districts (e.g., public utilities). If all else fails and you find yourself with no resource from which to develop your sample frame, you can use the random selection of telephone prefixes corresponding to specific neighborhoods.

Instrumentation. Surveys are only as good as the questions asked. Developing questions that measure the variables of interest and putting the instrument together to make it attractive to the respondent and to reflect "professional" appearance are important concerns. Designing questions that are not vague or misleading and keeping the instrument to the point help reduce respondent burden. In addition, the client should help in the pretest of the instrument. These strategies also help to achieve a good response rate.

Survey Costs. Survey data collection can be expensive. Major budget items for mail surveys include staff time, questionnaire printing, mailing (two or three rounds plus postcards), telephone work, coding and data entry, data processing, supplies and equipment, and possibly travel. As you can see, the number of cost items is expansive and, if you do not carefully plan for your costs, your budget can be easily depleted.

Scheduling. You need to anticipate all the delays that are inherent in survey data collection. If your staff has little prior experience, you should think in terms of 125% to 150% time inflation in data collection (Warwick & Lininger, 1975, p. 35). Surveys are also quite sensitive to holidays and community and city events. Establishing unrealistic timelines can lead to internal frustration (between you and other staff) and external disenchantment on the part of your client because you will not complete your data collection in a timely manner. Box 5.4 provides an example of detailed survey instructions, and Box 5.5 provides a method for monitoring survey returns (you will need to keep a master log; see Fowler, 1988). (For more detailed information on planning and budgeting, see Hedrick et al., 1992.)

Survey research can provide systematic data collection for a thorough examination. Nevertheless, there are strengths and weaknesses in this method of data collection. If you intend to describe and analyze an urban characteristic across a large population, survey research is the approach for you. With its capacity to elicit a wide range of responses and its sampling capabilities, you can reduce the bias in field research. The key in survey research, if you do not intend to interview the entire population but still want to generalize across the population, is in the sampling (i.e., random selection). Furthermore, mail and telephone surveys allow for anonymity and access.

Again, weaknesses exist. All surveys are costly and take time. If you try to overcome this limitation by conducting a quick survey, the cost to data collection can be a low response rate, thereby reducing the value of

BOX 5.4
Mail Survey Checklist

1. Number the master list (you need a set of mailing labels for the master list, each mail out, and each set of postcard reminders).

2. Number the labels very lightly in pencil. You must be very careful that these are numbered exactly the same as the master list.

3. Number the surveys in the space that says, "Mailing Number" in black ink.

4. Sign all of your cover letters personally or have someone do it by proxy rather than xerox with the signature. This gives it the "personal" touch. Use blue ink!

5. Label and stuff envelopes—survey, cover letter, and return envelope. It's necessary to keep a close eye on the label numbers and the survey numbers to make sure they match. After the stuffing, erase the penciled numbers, and seal the envelopes, unless your mailing department does that for you. [Here it is necessary for us to zip code sort before mailing—another thing to check with your mailing department.]

6. Note the day that you receive your first survey return in the mail and one week from that date mail your first class thank you/reminder postcards. One of your sets of labels will go on these and they will need to be stamped "First Class" in red ink. The ones you get back saying that the addresses are bad or that the forwarding order has expired can be marked-off on the master list.

7. Two weeks after you mail your postcards you should mail your second wave of surveys following steps 2 through 5 again with the following exceptions:

   2. & 3. Eliminate all survey numbers that have been marked-off on the master list.

   4. Instead of the original cover letter just a short follow-up note is needed.
   These surveys need to be stamped "second attempt to deliver" on the front.

8. Two weeks after you mail your second wave you should mail your third and hopefully final wave. Same as 7, only of course these will be stamped "third attempt to deliver" on the front.

Additional things to note during the survey period:

a. As surveys come back that have requested results of the survey, pull the label from the next set and put it on an envelope. Keep these in a separate box and they will be ready to go when a summary of findings is printed.

b. Cross off the labels or pull and toss them on the additional sets of labels as you code the returns onto your master list.

c. We usually code with different color highlighting markers:
   1. Red—surveys returned and filled out
   2. Blue—Take their names off list—didn't want to fill out
   3. Yellow—Survey returned and they want results of survey
   4. Pink—Cards were returned with bad addresses, too ill, retired, or some legitimate reason for not filling it out that would eliminate them from the total survey count.

BOX 5.5
Survey Fact Sheet

Title   _____
Location
Sample Size
Date of First Mailing
Date of First Return
Date Postcards Mailed
Number Bad Addresses
Number Complete Returns on First Mailing
Date of Second Mailing
Number Complete Returns on Second Mailing
Date of Third Mailing
Number Complete Returns on Third Mailing
Total Number of Completed Returns
Number of Results Requested
Date Results Were Mailed
Staff Working on Project

Created by Ruth Self, Administrative Coordinator, Division of Governmental Studies & Services

---

your findings. Furthermore, survey data collection is a difficult means of assessing change, transformation, or development, which are integral considerations in any analysis of the flux in urban phenomena. Other limitations are discussed by Fowler (1988, pp. 71-72).

Group Interviews. Group surveys are also useful data collection tools in applied urban research (see Moore, 1987; Stewart & Shamdasani, 1990; both are in this series). Several techniques are common, including focus groups, nominal groups, and the Delphi method. Focus groups and nominal groups are very useful when time is short or your respondents commonly meet in groups, such as in advisory boards, boards of directors, or the staff of community organizations. The Delphi technique can be either administered face-to-face over time or self-administered. Group techniques can be valuable when you are looking for consensus but require a skilled approach (e.g., facilitation skills, flipcharts, and room arrangements) for successful data collection.

SUMMARY

Data collection is both science and art. Regardless of the method, you must blend systematic searches, observations, and interviews with a generous dose of creativity. Signposts proclaiming "Your data are two more blocks this way" are rarely posted in urban research. You have to make connections; you have to "brainstorm" your sources. Also, data collection methods have different strengths and weaknesses. As a result, using multiple indicators and multiple methods for data collection allows for the triangulation of evidence and provides you with the most accurate picture possible.

EXERCISE

If you are working in groups, you have now identified your urban issue, thought strategically about how you would research it, and developed your most rigorous design and operationalized it. You are now ready for data collection. Although you have thought about the task in developing your design, you must now think about it in operational terms. Use the data collection strategies in this chapter to perform the following:

1. Find and assess five different secondary sources of data;
2. Identify and plan for doing the three types of field data collection; focus on what it would take to actually implement these data collection strategies (develop a task timeline);
3. Determine, as a research team, the criteria you would use to divide up the tasks.
   Do not forget to journal!

6

Reporting Your Research

This chapter provides an overview of reporting and includes both written and oral presentations of your research findings. Reporting must be compact, timely, user-friendly, and visually appealing to ensure that your results are heard and to enhance their potential for use. Getting applied urban research used requires careful planning to ensure that the right questions are asked and that findings are communicated in a language and format that potential users can easily understand. The chapter begins with a general discussion of factors that have been found to enhance the potential for utilization. Then we provide tips for enhancing the potential for utilization that can be integrated into the applied urban research process.

WHAT IS UTILIZATION?

Types of Utilization

Utilization is the ultimate goal of applied urban research. We undertake research projects to better understand urban processes and enhance the quality of life in our urban areas. But what is utilization? Carol Weiss has been in the forefront of developing our understanding of what research utilization is and how it occurs. In a study of more than 150 decision makers in the mental health field, Weiss found that utilization occurred when the research was of *high quality,* the findings could be *practically implemented*, the findings *conformed with the user's expectations,* the findings were *relevant to the user's work*, and whether and how much the findings *challenged current practices* (Weiss & Bucuvalas, 1980). Other research has shown that the client's information needs, decision characteristics, the political climate, and the availability of competing information can influence research utilization (e.g., Cousins & Leithwood, 1986).

Regarding how research gets used, a variety of models have been proposed, critiqued, and refined (e.g., Rieker, 1980; Rosenthal, 1980; Sunesson & Nilsson, 1988; Weiss, 1979; Yin & Andranovich, 1987). Weiss's general utilization categories describing the relationships between the researcher and policy maker tend to be the basis for much of this work. Her research categories (Weiss, 1979) are as follows:

- *Knowledge-driven* or conducted to gain knowledge
- *Problem solving* or providing evidence to help solve policy problems
- *Interactive* or combining with experience to provide solutions to policy problems
- *Political* or supporting predetermined positions or advocating
- *Tactical* or supporting immediate needs (e.g., prestige, delay)
- *Enlightenment* or helping to make better sense of the world for decision makers

The refinements tend to suggest that the nature of the information, the characteristics and needs of the policy maker (including the organizational context), the characteristics of the researcher, and the processes through which the information is transmitted all affect utilization. Typical of the recommendations to address barriers to the utilization of research are involving the client in the specification of the research design, involving the client in the operationalization of the research design, assisting in the interpretation of the research design and the research findings, and following up with the client as needed. These recommendations fit the applied research focus of maintaining a collaborative, problem-solving, and action-oriented research focus. Bringing new ideas or ways of approaching urban policy formation to policy makers is grounded in communication.

Tips for Communicating

Communication is a two-way process requiring the researcher to keep decision makers apprised of the constraints and realities of the research process as well as informed about how information may be useful in policy formation. Communication also is an important part of doing credible and relevant applied urban research.

The decision maker (the client) should let the researcher know the constraints and realities of his or her world. In addition, clients should keep the researcher informed about changes that are occurring that might affect the context of the research or the applicability of the findings (e.g., staff changes, new practice approaches). The importance of this point goes beyond having two-way interaction; it suggests that, to be successful, researchers and clients must rely on each other and work closely together.

Lessons from the many research utilization studies suggest some practical ways of enhancing utilization. Enhancing utilization potential begins early in the research process; thus the client should be involved in the strategic-thinking process. When brainstorming the various design alternatives, data sources, and analytical techniques, the client can be an important source of information. Knowing what efforts have preceded yours helps to fill in knowledge gaps and ground your research in the client's needs. You also will be provided with a certain amount of focus in terms of your objectives, approach and method, and reporting strategies. It is important to address all of the client's concerns, both procedural and substantive, to get your research used; after all, you must be responsive to the client's needs.

Some clients may want to review all data collection instruments or protocols. Even if a client does not, you should insist that he or she does. This simple practice keeps the client informed of what you are doing along the way, keeping the research project on the front burner while you are conducting it. Client review also helps build trust in the research as the client has the chance to clear up any questions prior to the presentation of the research findings. In addition, many programs have political goals as well as substantive goals. Applied urban research requires sensitivity to these nonresearch goals; all of this must be explicitly incorporated into your strategic calculus to enhance utilization potential.

Finally, it is critical to present your research in a timely manner; timely not only in meeting externally imposed deadlines, but also in providing clients with fast, quality information. As suggested in Chapter 3, full-blown research designs may have to yield to more adaptive ("quick and dirty") approaches. Again, the purpose, approach and method, and reporting strategies must address the client's needs, one of which is timeliness.

In sum, Weiss (1984) suggests the following steps to enhance the utilization of your research:

- Plan the research with the client in mind
- Stay close to the events being examined
- Concentrate on conditions that can be altered
- Make your reports clear, well-written, and timely
- Get the results out (disseminate)
- Fit your analysis into the big picture
- Maintain quality control over the research product to produce high quality work

COMMUNICATION FORMATS

If you have maintained close relations with the client throughout the research project, submitting a final report might seem like an easy thing to do. But *how* you present the results of your research is as important as the results themselves (see Ball & Anderson, 1977; McLaughlin, Weber, Covert, & Ingle, 1988). Table 6.1 illustrates the variety of reporting formats

Table 6.1

Communication Choices

	Reporting Format							
Audiences	Technical Report	Executive Summary	Update	Memo	News Release	Public Meeting	Staff Workshop	Videotape
Public agency								
Program administrator								
Other management staff								
Program providers								
City Council (other legislatures)								
Advisory committees								
Community groups								
Current clients								
Potential clients								
Professional organizations								
Media								

SOURCE: Adapted from Ball & Anderson, 1977.

available for use and provides a list of potential users of your research. If seen as a matrix, there are a variety of reporting formats, both written and otherwise, that can be used to present your research to the client.

Written Reports

A written report is one of the most common ways of organizing your research results. Written reports to clients tend to be organized differently than academic papers. The most important information (the research findings) should come first: If the reader had only 10 minutes to spend with your report, would the findings be found? Most research reports use an executive summary (an abstract of the most critical information in the report) to address the time constraints of the busy decision maker. In addition, in the body of the report, important information should always be provided at the beginning of the section or otherwise highlighted. The readability of the report is crucial to its reception. A report that contains a lot of jargon (specialized technical terms) is difficult to follow, and the importance of your message can get lost in translation. Many current word processing programs have a grammar check; MS Word includes a Fog index that alerts you to the overall level of jargon in your report. Your report should be written to address the practical needs of the client: Help the client implement your findings by suggesting alternatives. Examples of professional applied urban research reports can be obtained from your public agencies or might be available in your government repository library at the local university (e.g., HUD urban policy reports, environmental impact statements, *Budgets in Brief*).

Your report should be concise and to the point; do not pad the report with filler. When you write the report, consider using bullets to present information rather than paragraphs of text. There is nothing less appealing than a report that is text from margin to margin, top to bottom, front to back.

The use of maps, charts, diagrams, tables, and other visual aids is highly recommended. In applied urban research, maps and other visual aids should be keyed to the level of analysis used. Presenting maps of the metropolitan region will not help communicate findings about neighborhood-level after-school recreation programs in the inner city. Maps representing neighborhoods will not address regional topics such as the location of NIMBY facilities. These aids should be constructed and used with a sensitivity to the client's needs. Tufte (1983, 1990) is an excellent resource for illustrating how to use visual aids to enhance reporting presentation.

Other useful tips include submitting your report with a transmittal letter (see Box 6.1). The transmittal letter sets the context and highlights the critical information in the report, providing easy access to a potentially larger audience. Sometimes attaching a brief memo containing basically the same information as a transmittal letter is provided to facilitate the routing of the report within the client's organization.

Oral Presentations

In addition to submitting a written report, the client might ask you to provide verbal briefing. In this case, as with the written report, know the audience (e.g., managers, technical staff, the public). The level of technical information presented should match the audience's level of technical awareness. You should have a positive attitude and not speak down to the audience, but do not bore them with the details of the analysis; they can get these from the written report. Using visual aids (e.g., slides, overhead transparencies) is recommended, but make sure that you have made arrangement for the necessary equipment ahead of time. Also, it is important to involve the audience in the presentation. Asking questions that bring the audience "in" is useful; the questions should be positive and action-oriented rather than negative (e.g., "How many would like to see . . . ?"). You might allow questions during the presentation or ask the audience to hold questions until the end. Depending on the type of presentation, you might want to have a partner to help in the presentation (e.g., help with materials, record comments; see Moore, 1987, Ch. 9).

Facilitating oral presentations is not difficult, but it does require forethought (and experience always helps, especially with disruptive members of the audience). Here are some general tips for oral presentation (see Goad, 1982, for other examples of presentation planning, using active listening skills, and getting people involved).

- Depending on the size and type of audience, a brief warm-up can help bring the audience into the meeting (warm-ups vary from brief introductions to "What do you think of those Orioles?" types of questions).
- Share the agenda (and the time you plan to take) with the audience so that everyone knows what will be covered and when.
- Plan your presentation so that important information is provided first (after the warm-up and agenda).
- Alternate between talking and using visual aids.
- When possible, provide handouts of selected visual aids.

BOX 6.1
Transmittal Letter

Program for Local Government Education

Washington State University

509-335-7425

WSU-Cooperative Extension
411 Hulbert Hall
Pullman, WA 99164-6230

Division of Governmental Studies
and Services
Department of Political Science
Pullman, WA 99164-4870

March 1, 1991

TO: Local Government Growth Strategies Forum Participants

Policy Council
Local Government
Representatives:

Leo Fancey
City Manager
Sunnyside

Gail Hatfield
County Clerk
Pacific County

Nan Henriksen
Mayor
Camas

Joan LeMieux
County Commissioner
Cowlitz County

Gene Liddell
City Council Member
Lacey

Sandra Nourse-Madson
City Planner
Colville

Jim Rumpeltes
Administrator
Clallam County

Jack Westerman III
County Assessor
Jefferson County

FROM:

The strong interest in using cooperative conflict resolution techniques for growth management has become more important during the past year. Both the Growth Management Act of 1990 (SHB2929) and the recommendations of the Growth Strategies Commission make mediated dispute resolution an expected part of growth management in Washington state.

The enclosed report *Planning for Cooperation: Local Government Choices* by Jack Kartez outlines several approaches to collaborative dispute resolution in states with new growth management laws. Dr. Kartez, former associate professor of Environmental Science and Regional Planning at Washington State University, raises questions for state and local officials to explore as planning in the 1990s evolves in Washington.

This study is a product of the Renton Growth Strategies Forum sponsored by the Association of Washington Cities, the Washington State Association of Counties and the WSU Program for Local Government Education (PLGE) held in May 1990. The Growth Forum's purpose was to allow local officials in Washington to hear and learn from individuals working with highly diverse state growth management frameworks in four "bellwether" states: Georgia, Florida, Oregon and California.

One of the report's major findings is the pre-conflict planning and consensus building are effective steps for aiding the resolution of certain sharp conflicts when they do occur. The report focuses on the logic and features of different approaches used by city, county and state governments to resolve disputes and how jurisdictions can structure face-to-face cooperation. However, it doesn't catalog details of specific legislation, pretend to be a primer on land-use planning and intergovernmental law, or serve as a basic reference on alternative dispute resolution techniques.

PLGE is pleased to make this report available to you and others interested. Copies can be obtained by calling   at (509) 335-7425.

Cooperating Organizations: Association of Washington Cities, Washington State Association of Counties,
Washington Association of County Officials; Sponsored by a grant from the Kellogg Foundation
Program for Local Government Education services are available without discrimination

Disruptions are always a problem. Do not fight with or debate disruptive members. You can ask how much time is needed to air the concerns; when the disruptive members have finished, paraphrase their main points and thank them for contributing. If you are recording the meeting (writing down what people are saying on flipchart pages to retain ideas and limit repetition), include the disrupter's main points. If problems continue, survey the group for other reactions to the disruption—most groups will accept responsibility for their members. Finally, when you have finished (end by summarizing your main points), ask if there are any other questions from the audience.

SUMMARY

Presentation format is critical for enhancing the utilization potential of your research. Good reporting requires planning, knowing your audience, and effectively presenting important information. A communication format checklist was provided to help you address these concerns. Written reports and oral presentations were discussed and tips for making effective presentations, including dealing with disruptive members, were provided.

EXERCISE

You now have collected and analyzed the data on your urban issue. Next you need to consider how it will be presented and utilized. You want to increase the chances that your research will influence or help to improve the urban issue on which you have been working. Hence you must decide the best format and strategy for presentation to increase the potential of the research being used.

Break into teams (although you can again do this individually) and decide how your group will be able to increase your utilization possibilities. To get started, think of the utilization category your report will fit: Does this begin to identify your research's usefulness? What are some other reasons that make your report useful? It is not against the rules to build some of these reasons into the presentation.

Now plan for the actual communication format. You may be required to submit a written report and to make an oral presentation. Although these communication vehicles have similarities, they have different elements that require some additional, specialized planning. How will you organize each? What kind of visual aids will you need for the report? For the oral presentation? How will they be prepared and taken to the oral presentation site? How will you present your findings in an effective way? Who will your audience be and how does that shape your presentation format(s)? How can you make your presentation useful to your readers or listeners? These are just some of the questions you need to pose.

Once you have planned your presentation, practice executing the plan. Good luck!

7

Prospectus for Applied Urban Research

FUTURE ISSUES

We have suggested that applied urban research is a collaborative, problem-solving, and action-oriented approach that can help us make sense of the current changes in the urban system. By focusing on levels of analysis and paying close attention to how a given issue is viewed from different levels—and asking the questions, Who benefits from a given course of action or inaction? Who is harmed?—urban researchers can help illuminate the challenges facing urban areas.

The future of applied urban research will be outward-looking, examining particular urban issues in relation to other processes originating at different levels of the urban hierarchy. Resolving any given urban problem will require exploring new avenues and forging alternative solutions, some of which might require collaborating at spatial levels in which we do not currently have recognized authorities (e.g., the region). At the same time, the resolution of urban problems will need all of the available resources and capacity. This suggests renewing the action orientation of applied urban research with added creativity, bringing more of the people affected into the problem-solving process.

Substantively, applied urban research will focus on many of the same issues that have been noted throughout this text: the globalization and internationalization of the economy, quality-of-life issues, environmental concerns, and the capacity of urban authorities to resolve problems. Regarding globalization and internationalization, the changing relationship between politics and economics has seemingly diminished our capacities in cities to address urban problems effectively. The spheres of influence of nation-states, juxtaposed to the continuing globalization of the economy, have created a new schema of power, influence, and competition for neighborhoods and cities. This requires new analyses of how our cities will respond to urban problems as well as the linkages that will be employed to maintain or enhance their position in the hierarchy of the world system of cities. This prospect might seem quite abstract at first, but after closer inspection, it should illustrate the connection between local economic development, an important issue on the urban agenda, and a city's position in both the U.S. and global economies.

The growing diversity of our urban areas and the changing distribution of the employment base of many cities and regions have led to a resurfacing of difficult social problems. In the United States and elsewhere, the importance of borders in the global economy seems to be in question. One result has been compelling visual evidence of the disparity between rich and poor, with the middle class less evident in cities. As more and different people move to cities (immigrants and others looking for opportunities), issues of race and poverty will once again underlie our concerns for poor health care, the need to revamp public education and skills training in a dual labor market, and restricted economic and social mobility. The resource demands suggested by these urban issues are great, but bringing a greater number and more diverse group of affected people and organizations might help sharpen the problem-solving focus of urban authorities.

Quality-of-life issues, never far from the public consciousness, are being recast as urban issues. Health issues, such as community health and AIDS policy (see Slack, 1991), have already made their presence felt in heated debates in city council chambers and the corporate boardrooms of hospitals. Homelessness, an issue in most large cities across the United States, features an array of problems for cities affecting everyone, even those with homes. Likewise, housing has once again become a heated topic, where homelessness has been displaced by the problem of the rising costs of purchasing a home by the middle class. Related to the need to assess quality-of-life issues is the need to analyze the efforts of government programs that affect our quality of life. More specifically, applied urban research needs to focus on innovative responses at different levels of analysis to identify effective programs, assess what makes them effective, and provide alternative means to diffuse them to other locales. Even the mapping of these social concerns would improve the capacity of urban authorities to make informed decisions. Shannon, Pyle, and Bashshur's (1990) work on AIDS suggests some fruitful avenues.

Environmental concerns, waxing and waning in the United States since the 1970s, have skyrocketed back onto the urban agenda as cities and regions have witnessed decreasing landfill sites, complex groundwater problems, and seemingly little capacity to resolve these problems. Coupled with growth-management concerns (e.g., protecting unspoiled areas, managing development, and managing traffic flows), the environment promises to be a key urban issue in the next decade. Resolving environmental concerns, many of which are transboundary issues affecting several urban areas at the same time, will require using the regional level of analysis for problem solving and then for taking action at the regional level. In the United States, there are no common institutional arrangements for regional problem solving, although several states are moving to establish regional authorities (see Kartez, 1990).

In the face of these mounting urban issues, the debate over whether the United States should initiate a national urban policy is raising questions about intergovernmental responsibilities. The lack of a national urban policy has resulted not from a conspiracy, but from a market-oriented philosophy pursued by successive presidential regimes that has assumed that the best way to assist neighborhoods, cities, and regions is to reduce the presence of the federal government. Consequently, "fend for yourself federalism" has produced a different set of opportunities and constraints for cities. Little attention has been directed at this latest dimension of intergovernmental relations: local-local collaboration.

To assess the myriad questions that fall out of these broad substantive areas, researchers need to increase their comparative analysis skills and direct their attention to the regional level. The growing list of transboundary concerns requires new ways of thinking about collaborative problem solving. In this light, the regional level of analysis is likely to become a much more significant level of analysis.

Comparative analysis, the understanding of how other urban areas are responding to internal and external demands and what we could learn from the experiences of others, will be more in demand. The transference of lessons from one urban context to another must be done carefully, however. In earlier chapters, we pointed out the need to develop multiple indicators and a long-term understanding of urban processes to develop a clearer understanding of the implications of urban outcomes. In a recent book, Keating (1991) followed this path using the conceptual tool *urban regime* (discussed in Chapter 2 of this text). Keating's work provides an excellent model for thinking about and doing applied urban research, particularly given his focus on problem solving (termed *governing capacity* by Keating).

This reframing of urban issues will also demand a reframing of the conventional wisdom regarding response. In many parts of the United States we are witnessing greater public involvement in local decision making, with traditionally "closed systems" such as public health and safety being opened to the "community." One of the many issues facing applied urban research is the examination of jurisdictional boundaries from the perspective of enhanced regional coordination while maintaining local quality of life and community access to policy making.

THE APPLIED FOCUS

A book that expressly holds itself out as an applied guide for research that others should take stock in and draw upon must provide some explication of method. Yet our intention was not to simply mirror the standard methods books, as valuable as these texts are. Rather, our goal was to sift through the vast and complex area of urban inquiry—including our own experiences—in order to glean the essential elements of applied urban research, particularly techniques to conduct research. Thus you did not find a variety of statistical formulas, measures of association and prediction, or significance tests. What you did find were methods to break the research process down into manageable tasks and then the means to organize these tasks to address the purpose and to meet the needs of your project. We have provided various checklists and questions, but only as a method to encourage greater perception about your applied project. In no way is this intended to be an ironclad, by-the-numbers formula. Because of the variety of conditions and purposes you will face in the field, you need to have a set of guides for orientation; but good research also requires a sense of context and a toleration for spontaneity.

Most important, we remind you of two critical themes that bind the various points, lists, and questions together in the applied urban research process. First, strategic thinking underpins an effective research project. Granted, this exercise ought to occur before initiating a project, but it should continue throughout the entire process to picture tasks, their challenges, and your contingencies. In short, it forces you to frame and reframe your research activities and questions. In this way, you will sidestep many of the pitfalls that await you in doing urban research.

Second, we define applied urban research as a collaborative, problem-solving, response-oriented endeavor. In this light, we suggested throughout the text that the research process is a matter of purpose and need. Failing to draw early connections between these points may leave your activities and overall project adrift.

Whether we have accomplished our goals in this short text on applied urban research we leave to the reader's judgment.

References

Anderson, J. E. (1984). *Public policy making* (3rd ed.). New York: Holt, Rinehart & Winston.

Andranovich, G. (1991). *Regional policy management in a transborder setting.* Paper presented at annual meeting of the Urban Affairs Association, Vancouver, Canada.

Androit, D., Androit, J., & Androit, L. (1986). *Guide to U.S. government statistics.* McLean, VA: Documents Index.

Anton, T. J. (1989). *American federalism and public policy.* New York: Random House.

Babbie, E. (1989). *The practice of social research* (5th ed.). Belmont, CA: Wadsworth.

Balachandran, M. (1980). *Regional statistics: A guide to information resources.* Detroit: Gale Research.

Baldassare, M. (1986). *Trouble in paradise.* New York: Columbia University Press.

Ball, S., & Anderson, S. B. (1977, August). Dissemination, communication, and utilization. *Education and Urban Society, 9,* 457-470.

Barry, J., & Derevlany, J. (Eds.). (1987). *Yuppies invade my house at dinnertime.* Hoboken, NJ: Big River.

Beauregard, R. A. (Ed.). (1989a). *Atop the urban hierarchy.* Totowa, NJ: Rowman & Littlefield.

Beauregard, R. A. (Ed.). (1989b). *Economic restructuring and political response.* Newbury Park, CA: Sage.

Benjamin, R. L. C. (1984). From waterways to waterfronts. In R. D. Bingham & J. P. Blair (Eds.), *Urban economic development* (pp. 23-46). Beverly Hills, CA: Sage.

Blakely, E. J. (1979). *Community development research: Concepts, issues and strategies.* New York: Human Sciences Press.

Block, F. (1980). Beyond relative autonomy: State managers as historical subjects. *Socialist Register, 17,* 227-242.

Bluestone, B., & Harrison, M. (1981). *The deindustrialization of America.* New York: Basic Books.

Bollens, J. C., & Schmandt, H. J. (1975). *The metropolis* (2nd ed.). New York: Harper & Row.

Brewer, J., & Hunter, A. (1989). *Multimethod research.* Newbury Park, CA: Sage.

Browning, R. P., Marshall, D. R., & Tabb, D. H. (1984). *Protest is not enough.* Berkeley: University of California Press.

Campbell, D. T., & Stanley, J. (1966). *Experimental and quasi-experimental designs for research.* Chicago: Rand McNally.

Carney, J., Hudson, R., & Lewis, J. (Eds.). (1980). *Regions in crisis.* New York: St. Martin's.

Chase-Dunn, C. (1985). The system of world cities, A.D. 800-1975. In M. Timberlake (Ed.), *Urbanization in the world economy* (pp. 269-292). New York: Academic Press.

Clark, L. P. (1979). *Designs for evaluating social programs.* New York: Policy Studies Associates.

Clark, T. N. (1990). Series editor's introduction. In S. E. Clarke (Ed.), *Urban innovation and autonomy* (pp. 7-15). Newbury Park, CA: Sage.

Clarke, S. E. (Ed.). (1990). *Urban innovation and autonomy.* Newbury Park, CA: Sage.

Cook, T. D., & Campbell, D. T. (1979). *Quasi-experimentation: Design and analysis issues for field settings.* Chicago: Rand McNally.

Cooper, H. M. (1989). *Integrating research* (rev. ed.). Newbury Park, CA: Sage.

Cousins, J. B., & Leithwood, K. A. (1986, Fall). Current empirical research on evaluation utilization. *Review of Education Research, 56,* 331-364.

Davis, M. (1990). *City of quartz.* New York: Verso.

Dickinson, R. (1964). *City and region: A geographical interpretation.* London: Routledge & Kegan Paul.

Dillman, D. A. (1978). *Mail and telephone surveys.* New York: John Wiley.

Downs, A. (1981). *Neighborhoods and urban development.* Washington, DC: Brookings Institution.

Erie, S. P. (1992, June). How the urban west was won. *Urban Affairs Quarterly, 27,* 519-554.

Fetterman, D. M. (1989). *Ethnography: Step by step.* Newbury Park, CA: Sage.

Fowler, F. J., Jr. (1988). *Survey research methods* (rev. ed.). Newbury Park, CA: Sage.

Garreau, J. (1991). *Edge city.* Garden City, NY: Doubleday.

Goad, T. W. (1982). *Delivering effective training.* San Diego: University Associates.

Goffman, E. (1967). *The presentation of self in everyday life.* Garden City, NY: Doubleday.

Gordon, D. M. (1984). Capitalist development and the history of American cities. In W. Tabb & L. Sawers (Eds.)., *Marxism and the metropolis* (pp. 21-53). Oxford, UK: Oxford University Press.

Gottdiener, M. (1985). *The social production of urban space.* Austin: University of Texas Press.

Gottdiener, M. (Ed.). (1986). *Cities in stress.* Beverly Hills, CA: Sage.

Gottdiener, M. (1987). *The decline of urban politics.* Newbury Park, CA: Sage.

Gottdiener, M., & Feagin, J. R. (1988, December). The paradigm shift in urban sociology. *Urban Affairs Quarterly, 24,* 163-187.

Gottdiener, M., & Pickvance, C. (Eds.). (1991). *Urban life in transition.* Newbury Park, CA: Sage.

Green, C. (1985). *Elitism vs. democracy in community organizations.* Bristol, IN: Wyndham Hall.

Hall, P. (1984). *The world cities* (3rd ed.). New York: St. Martin's.

Harrington, M. (1963). *The other America.* New York: Penguin.

Harrison, M. (1987). *Diagnosing organizations.* Newbury Park, CA: Sage.

Harvey, D. (1989). *The condition of postmodernism.* Oxford, UK: Basil Blackwell.

Hawley, W. D., et al. (1976). *Theoretical perspectives on urban politics.* Englewood Cliffs, NJ: Prentice-Hall.

Hedrick, T., Bickman, L., & Rog, D. J. (1992). *Planning applied research.* Newbury Park, CA: Sage.

Henderson, J., & Castells, M. (Eds.). (1987). *Global restructuring and territorial development.* Newbury Park, CA: Sage.

Henig, J. (1982). *Neighborhood mobilization.* New Brunswick, NJ: Rutgers University Press.

Henry, G. T. (1990). *Practical sampling.* Newbury Park, CA: Sage.

Herson, L. J. R., & Bolland, J. M. (1990). *The urban web.* Chicago: Nelson-Hall.

Herzog, L. A. (Ed.). (1986). *Planning the international border metropolis.* San Diego: Center for U.S.-Mexican Studies, University of California, San Diego.

Hiss, T. (1990). *The experience of place.* New York: Knopf.

Hoch, C., & Slayton, R. A. (1989). *New homeless and old.* Philadelphia: Temple University Press.

Hoffman, J. E. (1980). Problems of access in the study of social elites and boards of directors. In W. B. Shaffir, R. A. Stebbins, & A. Turowetz (Eds.), *Fieldwork experience* (pp. 45-56). New York: St. Martin's.

Hogwood, B. W., & Gunn, L. A. (1984). *Policy analysis for the real world.* New York: Oxford University Press.

Hoover, K. R. (1988). *The elements of social scientific thinking* (4th ed.). New York: St. Martin's.

Horowitz, R. (1983). *Honor and the American dream.* New Brunswick, NJ: Rutgers University Press.

Inter-University Consortium for Social and Political Research. (1988). *1987-1988 annual report.* Ann Arbor: University of Michigan.

Jones, C. O. (1984). *An introduction to the study of public policy* (3rd ed.). Belmont, CA: Brooks/Cole.

Jorgensen, D. L. (1989). *Participation observation.* Newbury Park, CA: Sage.

Kantor, P., & David, S. (1988). *The dependent city.* Glenview, IL: Scott, Foresman.

Karp, D. A. (1980). Observing behavior in public places: Problem and strategies. In W. B. Shaffir, R. A. Stebbins, & A. Turowetz (Eds.), *Fieldwork experience* (pp. 82-97). New York: St. Martin's.

Kartez, J. (1990). *Planning for cooperation.* Pullman: Program for Local Government Education, Washington State University.

Keating, M. (1991). *Comparative urban politics.* Brookfield, VT: Edward Elgar.

Kimmel, A. J. (1988). *Ethics and values in applied research.* Newbury Park, CA: Sage.

King, A. D. (1990). *Global cities.* New York: Routledge.

Kirby, A. (Ed.). (1992). *The pentagon and the cities.* Newbury Park, CA: Sage.

Knox, P. (1991). The restless urban landscape. *Annals of the Association of American Geographers, 8*(2), 181-209.

Lake, R. W. (1983). *Readings in urban analysis.* Rutgers, NJ: Center for Urban Policy Research, Rutgers University.

Lasswell, H. D. (1938). *Politics: Who gets what, when and how.* New York: McGraw-Hill.

Lawson, R. (Ed.). (1986). *The tenant movement in New York City: 1904-1984.* New Brunswick, NJ: Rutgers University Press.

Lerner, D., & Lasswell, H. D. (Eds.). (1951). *The policy sciences.* Stanford, CA: Stanford University Press.

Levy, F., Meltsner, A., & Wildavsky, A. (1974). *Urban outcomes.* Berkeley: University of California Press.

Lineberry, R. (1984). Mandating urban equality: The distribution of municipal public services. In H. Hahn & C. Levine (Eds.), *Readings in urban politics* (pp. 184-211). New York: Longman.

Lineberry, R., & Sharkansky, I. (1978). *Urban politics and public policy.* New York: Harper & Row.

Lipsey, M. (1990). *Design sensitivity.* Newbury Park, CA: Sage.

Lofland, J. (1984). *Analyzing social settings.* Belmont, CA: Wadsworth.

Majchrzak, A. (1984). *Methods for policy research.* Beverly Hills, CA: Sage.

Manheim, J. B., & Rich, R. C. (1986). *Empirical political analysis* (2nd ed.). New York: Longman.

Marin, G., & Marin, B. V. (1991). *Research with Hispanic populations.* Newbury Park, CA: Sage.

Mark, M. M., & Cook, T. D. (1984). Designing randomized experiments and random experiments. In L. Rutman (Ed.), *Evaluation research methods* (pp. 65-120). Newbury Park, CA: Sage.

Mark, M. M., & Shotland, R. L. (1987). Alternative models for the use of multiple methods. In M. M. Mark & R. L. Shotland (Eds.), *Multiple methods in program evaluation. New Directions of Program Evaluation, 35.* San Francisco: Jossey-Bass.

Markusen, A. (1987). *Regions.* Totowa, NJ: Rowman & Littlefield.

Mayer, N. S. (1984). *Neighborhood organizations and community development.* Washington, DC: Urban Institute.

McLaughlin, J. A., Weber, L. J., Covert, R. W., & Ingle, R. B. (Eds.). (1988). *Evaluation utilization. New directions in program evaluation, 39.* San Francisco: Jossey-Bass.

Meehan, E. J. (1988). *The thinking game.* Chatham, NJ: Chatham House.

Meltzer, J. (1984). *Metropolis to metroplex.* Baltimore, MD: Johns Hopkins University Press.

Mendenso, A. A. (1986). Yardsticks for measuring the success of service programs in Savannah. *State & Local Government Review, 18,* 89-92.

Mladenka, K. R. (1989, June). The distribution of urban public service. *Urban Affairs Quarterly, 24,* 556-583.

Moore, C. M. (1987). *Group techniques for idea building.* Newbury Park, CA: Sage.

Morgan, D. R. (1989). *Managing urban America* (3rd ed.). Belmont, CA: Brooks/Cole.

Morgan, G. (1986). *Riding the waves of change.* San Francisco: Jossey-Bass.

Murphy, T. P. (1980). *Urban indicators: A guide to information resources.* Detroit: Gale Research.

Nachmias, D., & Nachmias, C. (1990). *Research methods in social science* (3rd ed.). New York: St. Martin's.

Neiman, M. (1975). *Metropology.* Beverly Hills, CA: Sage.

Neiman, M., & Lovell, C. (1981, Spring). Mandating as a policy issue: The definitional problem. *Policy Studies Journal, 9,* 667-681.

Neiman, M., & Lovell, C. (1982, November). Federal and state mandating: A first look at the mandate terrain. *Administration & Society, 14,* 343-372.

Noyelle, T. J., & Stanback, T. M. (1983). *The economic transformation of American cities.* Totowa, NJ: Rowman & Allanheld.

Pahl, R. E. (1975). *Whose city* (2nd ed.). London: Penguin.

Palumbo, D. J. (Ed.). (1987). *The politics of program evaluation.* Newbury Park, CA: Sage.

Patton, C. V., & Sawicki, D. S. (1986). *Basic methods of policy analysis and planning.* Englewood Cliffs, NJ: Prentice-Hall.

Patton, M. Q. (1986). *Utilization focused evaluation* (2nd ed.). Newbury Park, CA: Sage.

Perry, S. (1987). *Communities on the way.* Albany: State University of New York Press.

Peterson, P. E., Rabe, B. G., & Wong, K. K. (1986). *When federalism works.* Washington, DC: Brookings Institution.

Peterson, P. E. (1981). *City limits.* Chicago: University of Chicago Press.

Pivo, G., & Rose, D. (1991). *Toward growth management monitoring in Washington state.* Olympia: Washington State Institute for Public Policy, Evergreen State College.

Portes, A., & Rumbaut, R. G. (1990). *Immigrant America.* Berkeley: University of California Press.

Posner, J. (1980). Urban anthropology: Fieldwork in semi-familiar settings. In W. B. Shaffir, R. A. Stebbins, & A. Turowetz (Eds.), *Fieldwork experience* (pp. 203-211). New York: St. Martin's.

Putt, A. D., & Springer, J. F. (1989). *Policy research: Concepts, methods, and applications.* Englewood Cliffs, NJ: Prentice-Hall.

Rieker, E. (1980, December). Evaluation research. *Knowledge, 2,* 215-236.

Riposa, G. (1991). *The political incorporation of Cambodians in California.* Paper presented at annual meeting of the American Political Science Association, Washington, DC.

Riposa, G., & Andranovich, G. (1988). Economic development policy: Whose interests are being served? *Urban Resources, 5*(1), 25-34.

Riposa, G., & Dersch, C. G. (1990). *Urban street gangs as political actors.* Paper presented at annual meeting of the American Political Science Association, San Francisco.

Riposa, G., & Dersch, C. G. (Eds.). (1992). *City of angels.* Dubuque, IA: Kendall/Hunt.

Riposa, G., & Slack, J. D. (1986). *Economic revitalization in small Texas cities.* Lubbock: Center for Public Service, Texas Tech University.

Rosenthal, R. (1984). *Meta-analytic procedures for social research.* Beverly Hills, CA: Sage.

Rosenthal, S. R. (1980, September). Providing analytic capacity for local urban policy. *Knowledge, 2,* 27-58.

Rossi, P. H., & Freeman, H. E. (1989) *Evaluation* (4th ed.). Newbury Park, CA: Sage.

Salant, P. (1990). *A community researcher's guide to rural data.* Covelo, CA: Island Press.

Sassen, S. (1991). *The global city.* Princeton, NJ: Princeton University Press.

Saunders, P. (1981). *Social theory and the urban question.* London: Hutchinson.

Schatzman, L., & Strauss, A. L. (1973). *Field research.* Englewood Cliffs, NJ: Prentice-Hall.

Shanahan, E. (1991, August). Going it jointly. *Governing, 4,* 70-76.

Shannon, G. W., Pyle, G. F., & Bashshur, R. L. (1990). *The geography of AIDS.* New York: Guilford.

Shively, W. P. (1980). *The craft of political research* (2nd ed.). Englewood Cliffs, NJ: Prentice-Hall.

Shively, W. P. (1984). *The research process in political science.* Itasca, IL: F. E. Peacock.

Sieber, J. (1992). *Ethically responsible research.* Newbury Park, CA: Sage.

Slack, J. D. (1991). *AIDS and the public workforce.* Tuscaloosa: University of Alabama Press.

Smith, M. P. (1988). *City, state, and market.* New York: Basil Blackwell.

Smith, M. P., & Feagin, J. R. (1987). Cities and the new international division of labor: An overview. In M. P. Smith & J. R. Feagin (Eds.), *The capitalist city* (pp. 3-34). New York: Basil Blackwell.

Smith, N. (1979, October). Toward a theory of gentrification. *Journal of the American Planning Association, 45,* 538-548.

Sorkin, M. (Ed.). (1992). *Variations on a theme park.* New York: Noonday.

Spector, M. (1980). Learning to study public figures. In W. B. Shaffir, R. A. Stebbins, & A. Turowetz (Eds.), *Fieldwork experience* (pp. 98-109). New York: St. Martin's.

Stewart, D. W. (1984). *Secondary research.* Beverly Hills, CA: Sage.

Stewart, D. W., & Shamdasani, P. N. (1990). *Focus groups.* Newbury Park, CA: Sage.

Stone, C. N. (1987). The study of the politics of urban development. In C. Stone & H. Sanders (Eds.), *The politics of urban development* (pp. 3-22). Lawrence: University of Kansas Press.

Stone, C. N. (1989). *Regime politics.* Lawrence: University of Kansas Press.

Stone, C. N., & Sanders, H. (Eds.) (1987). *The politics of urban development.* Lawrence: University of Kansas Press.

Sundeen, R. A. (1989). Volunteer participation in local government agencies. *Journal of Urban Affairs, 11*(2), 155-167.

Sunesson, S., & Nilsson, K. (1988, December). Explaining research utilization. *Knowledge, 10,* 140-155.

Tabb, W. K., & Sawers, L. (Eds.). (1984). *Marxism and the metropolis* (2nd ed.). Oxford, UK: Oxford University Press.

Timberlake, M. (Ed.). (1985). *Urbanization in the world economy.* New York: Academic Press.

Tufte, E. (1983). *The visual display of quantitative information.* Cheshire, CT: Graphics Press.

Tufte, E. (1990). *Envisioning information.* Cheshire, CT: Graphics Press.

Walton, J., & Masotti, L. (Eds.). (1976). *The city in comparative perspective.* Newbury Park, CA: Sage.

Warwick, D. P., & Lininger, C. A. (1975). *The sample survey.* New York: McGraw-Hill.

Waste, R. (Ed.). (1986). *Community power.* Beverly Hills, CA: Sage.

Waste, R. (1989). *The ecology of city policy making.* New York: Oxford University Press.

Weiss, C. H. (1972). *Evaluation research.* Englewood Cliffs, NJ: Prentice-Hall.

Weiss, C. H. (1979, September-October). The many meanings of research utilization. *Public Administration Review, 39,* 426-431.

Weiss, C. H. (1984). Increasing the likelihood of influencing decisions. In L. Rutman (Ed.), *Evaluation research methods* (pp. 159-190). Beverly Hills, CA: Sage.

Weiss, C. H., & Bucuvalas, M. J. (1980). *Social science research and decision making.* New York: Columbia University Press.

Welch, S., & Comer, J. (1988). *Quantitative methods for public administration* (2nd ed.). Homewood, IL: Dorsey.

Williams, O. P. (1971). *Metropolitan political analysis.* New York: Free Press.

Yates, D. (1980). *The ungovernable city* (4th ed.). Cambridge: MIT Press.

Yin, R. K. (1989). *Case study research* (rev. ed.). Newbury Park, CA: Sage.

Yin, R. K., & Andranovich, G. D. (1987). *Utilization of research in the natural hazards field.* Washington, DC: COSMOS Corporation.

Zehner, R. B., & Chapin, F. S., Jr. (1974). *Across the city line.* Lexington, MA: D. C. Heath.

Index

About the Authors

Gregory D. Andranovich is a political scientist at California State University, Los Angeles. He received his B.A. (1978) from Clinch Valley College and Ph.D. (1984) from the University of California, Riverside. He has worked for the U.S. General Accounting Office and COSMOS Corporation, and as a Local Government Specialist at Washington State University. His research interests are urban economic development policy making, regional policy management, and cross-cultural management in the public sector.

Gerry Riposa is Associate Professor of Political Science at California State University, Long Beach. He received his Ph.D. from the University of California, Riverside, in 1985. Along with teaching, he has worked in local government and served as a consultant on economic development projects and programs to reduce urban street gang violence. His publications have appeared in *Policy Studies Review, Policy Studies Journal,* and *Western Political Quarterly.* He is coeditor of *City of Angels* (1992). His research interests include urban economic development, urban street gangs, and policy implementation.

The authors have collaborated on several projects in the past, and their work has appeared in *Urban Resources, American Review of Public Administration, Texas Journal of Political Studies,* and the *Handbook of Comparative and Development Public Administration.*

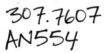